What Do We Do Now?

A WORKBOOK FOR
THE PRESIDENT-ELECT

Stephen Hess

Brookings Institution Press

Washington, D.C.

ABOUT BROOKINGS

The Brookings Institution is a private nonprofit organization devoted to research, education, and publication on important issues of domestic and foreign policy. Its principal purpose is to bring the highest quality independent research and analysis to bear on current and emerging policy problems. Interpretations or conclusions in Brookings publications should be understood to be solely those of the authors.

Library of Congress Cataloging-in-Publication data

Hess, Stephen.
   What do we do now? : a workbook for the president-elect / by Stephen Hess.
     p.   cm.
   Includes bibliographical references and index.
   Summary: "A workbook to guide future chief executives, decision by decision, through the minefield of transition. Based on experiences of a White House staffer and presidential adviser, shows what can be done to make presidential transitions go smoothly"—Provided by publisher.
   ISBN 978-0-8157-3655-4 (pbk. : alk. paper)
   1. Presidents—United States. 2. Presidents—United States—Transition periods. 3. Presidents—United States—Staff. I. Title.
   JK516.H45 2008
   352.230973—dc22   2008033786

9 8 7 6 5 4 3 2

The paper used in this publication meets minimum requirements of the American National Standard for Information Sciences—Permanence of Paper for Printed Library Materials: ANSI Z39.48-1992.

Design and composition by Naylor Design, Inc., Washington, D.C.
Printed by Versa Press, East Peoria, Illinois

Contents

may not have been Rhodes scholars, as were fifteen in the Kennedy administration, but many had been there six or eight years and knew a great deal about how government works. The Kennedy people might have gained from listening more.

I returned to work in the White House in 1969, after Nixon unexpectedly invited my good friend Daniel Patrick Moynihan to be the assistant to the president for urban affairs. Pat urged me to join him, and I became the deputy assistant. Working with Pat would have been a joy whatever the circumstances, but I also felt that Democrat Moynihan needed me to interpret the ways of Republicans who were to be his colleagues. During the transition, Pat was charged with creating a new White House unit, the Urban Affairs Council. In contrast to the gap between Kennedy and Eisenhower people in 1960, Moynihan knew not only the outgoing president's staff (he had been an assistant secretary of labor in the Johnson administration) but also the right people in the civil service. All accidental, perhaps, but also ideal: as a result, President Nixon was able to sign an executive order creating the Urban Affairs Council as his first act.

My next transition experience was more surprising. I had joined the Brookings Institution in 1972, with occasional short side trips back into government to help President Gerald Ford. On December 11, 1976, John Osborne wrote in his *New Republic* column, "Stephen Hess, a former Nixon assistant and Brookings Institution Fellow whose new book, *Organizing the Presidency,* was favorably mentioned in this space, learned on Friday, November 19, how personally and directly Carter is involved [in the transition]. Hess is a member of the U.S. delegation to the current session of the UN General Assembly. He was in his office at U.S. delegation headquarters in New York when a secretary told him that a Governor Carter was on the telephone. 'Governor Carter?' Hess said. 'I don't know any Governor Carter.' The secretary said it was *the* Governor Carter."

This is the sort of response, I later said, that must happen all the time when a president-elect calls folks who are not expecting to hear from him. For two months I gladly took Carter's calls (even when they were in the middle of Redskins games) and tried to answer his questions. "Should the Office of Special Representative for Trade Negotiations be taken out of the Executive Office of the President and put in the Treasury Department?" (No, it works well where it is; moving it would produce a prolonged fight.) Carter and his assistants were unfailingly polite and appreciative of my advice, and since I had been the editor-in-chief of the Republican platform I was grateful to have had their attention and goodwill. (My memos to President-elect Carter are reproduced in the 2002 edition of *Organizing the Presidency*.)

In 1980, the year Carter lost his bid for reelection to Ronald Reagan, planning for a presidency before a candidate gets elected became standard operating procedure. Carter made a worthy try in 1976, but it proved counterproductive when it led to an embarrassing conflict between his transition staff and his campaign staff. This might have been an object lesson for the out-of-office Republicans. Whatever the case, the work of Edwin Meese for candidate Reagan, the efforts of Ed Feulner's Heritage Foundation in creating a conservative agenda, and the logistical support of Bill Brock, the most creative Republican national chairman since Mark Hanna, produced what is now considered the gold standard for transition planning. My contribution, requested by Brock, was to outline necessary elements of putting together a transition. (The memo is reproduced in the 2002 edition of *Organizing the Presidency*.)

Transitions benefit greatly from the advice of think tanks, those not-for-profit centers doing public policy analysis that the government ought to be doing if it had the time and energy. A testament to their unique contribution to organizing knowledge is the steady stream of foreigners who trek to the Brookings Institution and other leading Washington think tanks for advice on how to start such centers in their own countries. In the Reagan-to-Bush transition (1988–89), I was part of a team convened by the National Academy of Public Administration, which produced *The Executive Presidency: Federal Management for the 1990s*. The panel included William T. Coleman Jr., Stuart E. Eizenstat, Fred F. Fielding, Andrew J. Goodpaster, Donald Rumsfeld, and Brent Scowcroft. Chaired by Elmer B. Staats, a former comptroller general of the United States, the panel focused on relations between careerists and political appointees and other public service concerns that were less likely to be at the top of the president-elect's political agenda.

Four years later, during the Bush-to-Clinton transition (1992–93), I was part of a team convened by the Carnegie Endowment for International Peace and the Peterson Institute for International Economics. The team, chaired by Richard C. Holbrooke, included Morton I. Abramowitz, Madeleine K. Albright, Frank C. Carlucci, Kenneth M. Duberstein, William Frenzel, Paul H. O'Neill, Peter G. Peterson, Elliot L. Richardson, and Theodore C. Sorensen. While our *Memorandum to the President-Elect* contained a wide range of suggestions, its primary one was that the White House establish a "three-council system" consisting of the National Security Council, the Economic Council, and the Domestic Council. The president accepted our recommendation.

Eight years later, during the Clinton-to-Bush transition (2000–01), the Presidential Appointee Initiative at Brookings, under the direction of Paul C. Light, produced the most thorough investigation, with recommendations, of the failings of the presidential appointments process. My contribution can be found in *Innocent until Nominated,* edited by G. Calvin Mackenzie (Brookings, 2001).

This slim volume is my attempt at keeping the record of my life in transitions intact in 2008.

GETTING STARTED

"The President needs help!"

These are the four most urgent words ever delivered to a president of the United States. They were the words of the President's Committee on Administrative Management. The president was Franklin Roosevelt, the year 1937. That was the year Inauguration Day was advanced from March 4 to January 20—and life for newly elected presidents became ever more difficult. You could no longer take a leisurely four months to plan your administration or, like Woodrow Wilson, enjoy a month's vacation in Bermuda.

Instead, following election on November 4, you have seventy-seven-and-a-half days (counting Christmas and New Year's Day) to perform the incredibly difficult and complex job of creating a government before taking office.

| CHAPTER 1 | # Getting Started |

There is no shadow cabinet to move in with you, as in a parliamentary system. Your staff—created for campaigning, not governing—lacks many of the talents you now require. Your political party asks not what it can do for you. The government's civil service is either too liberal or too conservative, according to past presidents. And this is just the start of your problems.

No political scientist so thoroughly understood the hazards of presidential transitions as Richard E. Neustadt, the Harvard professor who had also been on President Harry S. Truman's staff and an adviser to John F. Kennedy. The two primary hazards, writes Neustadt, are "newness," which he equates with ignorance, and "hubris," which he calls "a kind of early arrogance." The arrogance radiates from the winning team luxuriating in its remarkable victory. Counterarrogance can wait for your first defeat in Congress or your administration's first front-page scandal.

But ignorance? Surely we elect presidents of fine education, many skills, and experience in jobs with titles like "governor" or "senator." Yet governors too quickly learn that Washington is not Atlanta, Little Rock, or Austin writ large. It will take time and attention to unlearn lessons that had previously worked so well. As a senator, on the other hand, you have the right to believe that you know Washington. But what you soon realize is that the Washington you know largely revolves around Capitol Hill and its legislative ways. There are vast differences in scope and style between life under Article I and Article II.

As if to make this point brutally, Neustadt cites the experience of John F. Kennedy, the last senator elected president before the 2008 election. Less than three months after his inauguration, Kennedy blundered into the "misadventure at Cuba's Bay of Pigs in April 1961." In asking the Joint Chiefs of Staff for its assessment of the CIA's invasion plan, says Neustadt, Kennedy

evidently was too ignorant to understand that when the military is asked
to comment on an operation that is
someone else's responsibility it will
be loath to open its mind—or its
mouth. Nor did Kennedy understand
the terms of reference in which military advice was tendered to him. The
Joint Chiefs told him that they
thought the CIA plan had a "fair"
chance of success. What the colonel
who wrote those words meant by
them was "fair" as next to "poor."
What Mr. Kennedy took them to
mean was "fair" as "pretty good". . . .
And so it went. The military chiefs
were half a generation older than the
President: they had seen him on television during the campaign, champi-
oning vigor and calling for firmness
against Cuba. They did not wish to
look weak.

The transitions of the eight presidents-elect of the "modern" era have
been a mixed success at best. The
scholars' consensus is that two made
multiple mistakes so serious as to cast
doubt on whether they were ready for prime time. By their actions (or
inaction) they dug holes for themselves that they would have to dig
out of. Digging takes time and resources. Two presidents allowed
events to go forward that had lasting adverse international consequences. All made errors—most often in appointments, though sometimes in policy proposals as well—for which they paid a price.

While you were campaigning, some folks—volunteers, interns,
staff—were gathering material for your use after the election. This
probably included job descriptions for positions you will have to fill,
an annotated list of laws that will expire during your first year in office,

The seal used on page 1 is from the invitation
to the inaugural ceremony of President Richard
Nixon in 1969. It is the Great Seal of the United States, not the Seal of the President. The
Great Seal was approved by the Continental
Congress in 1782. The Seal of the President is
a product of tradition, not statute, and dates
back to President Rutherford B. Hayes, 1877.

The difference between the two seals is
slight. The Great Seal features a circle of clouds
encasing thirteen stars above the eagle; the
Seal of the President has an arced cornea of
thirteen stars with the clouds above. Until 1945,
however, there was a more radical difference.
The eagle in the Great Seal held an olive branch
in its right talon and a bundle of arrows in the
left. This was reversed in the president's seal by
Harry Truman. As explained in a White House
press release: "In the new Coat of arms, Seal
and Flag, the Eagle not only faces to its right—
the direction of honor—but also toward the olive branches of peace which it holds in its right
talon. Formerly the eagle faced toward the arrows in its left talon—arrows, symbolic of war."

and documentation on turning campaign promises into draft legislation or executive orders. Your experts have contributed memos of what awaits you in the Middle East, Africa, Latin America, and other places, as well as how to fix the health care system and the economy.

It used to be that pre-election planning was considered bad politics: you don't want voters to feel that you're taking them for granted. But Jimmy Carter experienced no adverse electoral consequences when he created a small transition office in Atlanta during the 1976 campaign. What he faced instead was a hammer-and-tong battle between transition staff and campaign staff. This happened again after Bill Clinton's 1992 victory. Ronald Reagan, however, devised a formula that worked well: leave no room for infighting by giving the ultimate power to a member of your inner circle whose decisions are understood to have your full support.

Why this book is called "What Do We Do Now?"

The title of this book—suggested by my friend and former Nixon speechwriter William Safire—comes from the 1972 movie *The Candidate*. Written by Jeremy Larner, himself a former political speechwriter, the movie stars Robert Redford as Bill McKay, the politically disillusioned son of California's former governor. McKay is persuaded to launch a long-shot candidacy for a seat in the U.S. Senate. In the early months of the campaign, McKay attempts to discuss substantive issues with voters. But as he gains in the polls, McKay drops his focus on issues for empty slogans such as "For a better way: Bill McKay!" In the movie's famous closing scene, McKay—unexpectedly victorious and facing the prospect of going to Washington—confronts his campaign manager with the question "What do we do now?" The line has come to symbolize the idea that politicians often care more about getting elected than about governing.

McKay's question actually has a shadow in history. According to Arthur M. Schlesinger Jr., when candidate John F. Kennedy asked adviser Clark Clifford in August 1960 to write a transition memo, he said, "If I am elected, I don't want to wake up on the morning of November 9 and have to ask myself, 'What in the world do I do now?'"

To supplement the material you may receive from these and other quarters, this workbook offers some thoughts on how to best organize a presidency distilled from accumulated wisdom and experience. It contains no flight plans for how to deal with Iraq or the economy. Instead it draws on the excellent work of scholars who professionally study presidential transitions and on my own involvement in all of the transitions since 1960–61, when I was a young man on President Dwight Eisenhower's White House staff awaiting the arrival of the incoming Kennedy people.

Presidential experts do not always agree, of course. One school of transition scholars advocates that you "hit the ground running." They urge you to take advantage of the honeymoon period that the media and the voters usually give a new president. You'll never have all the pieces in place when you take office anyway, so go for quick victories. Good first impressions are important. Another school of scholars advises you to be cautious while you're still learning the ropes. You'll never have all the pieces in place when you take office, and ignorant presidents make unnecessary mistakes. It's hard to undo bad first impressions.

Both are right.

After you have assessed your circumstances—the size of your electoral victory, makeup of Congress, state of the economy, immediate troubles in the world—it is essential to prioritize your long-term goals and then have a pocketful of doable actions ready for quick victories.

Now, let us begin.

Transition Budget

The federal government provides funds for both the incoming and outgoing presidents under the Presidential Transition Act. The funds cover office space, staff compensation, communications services, and printing and postage costs relating to the transition. During the 2000–01 transition, the General Services Administration (GSA, the housekeeping arm of government) was authorized to spend $7.1 million—$1.83 million for the outgoing Clinton administration, $4.27 million for the incoming George W. Bush administration, and an additional $1 million for the GSA to provide additional assistance. Had there been a presidential transition in 2004–05, a total of $7.7 million would have been authorized. Funds for the 2008–09 transition will be provided for in the president's fiscal 2009 budget.

Source: Congressional Research Service.

Worksheets

Properly position your presidency—creating a sort of personal political gyroscope—by completing these two short exercises. First, list the five reasons you think people voted for you (not merely what your pollster told you). Then list the five most important promises you made during the campaign. Don't include promises such as President Jimmy Carter's "I'll never lie to you."

If you think people voted for you because of your personal characteristics and to deny the Oval Office to your opponent or his party, then you have already accomplished these goals. But the other reasons you wrote down probably relate to fears and hopes at home and abroad. Refer to this list every December when you start to write your State of the Union address.

As for promises you made during the campaign, some will obviously have to be honored over time, but others should be ready for submission to Congress (or to be put into effect as executive orders) as soon as possible after the inauguration. Keep the list short and doable. You can name on the fingers of one hand the things Ronald Reagan said he wanted to do in January 1981. While you want to keep your promises, you may find that circumstances change and you have to adjust to new situations. Or you may learn things you didn't know, as happened with President Kennedy, who had spoken of a "missile gap"—a Soviet advantage in nuclear weapons capabilities that threatened U.S. security—during the 1960 campaign. Later evidence revealed the missile gap to be a myth.

If President-elect Bill Clinton had used these exercises in 1992, he might have avoided the rocky start of his administration when it got sidetracked by the "gays in the military" issue.

Why Did the Voters Choose You?

1. _____

2. _____

3. _____

4. _____

5. _____

What Promises Did You Make?

1. _____

2. _____

3. _____

4. _____

5. _____

Article 125 of the Uniform Code of Military Justice bans homosexual behavior in the armed forces. Bill Clinton pledged during the 1992 campaign to lift the ban unconditionally. In response to a question during a press conference on November 16, 1992, the president-elect declared, "I intend to press forward with that in an expeditious way early in the term." Although Clinton's campaign had been built on economic recovery, tax policy, budget cuts—"It's the economy, stupid!"—the first weeks of his presidency ended up being dominated by gays in the military.

The emotional nature of the issue caught the new president unprepared. Responses were instantaneous and explosive. In his memoirs, *My Life* (Knopf, 2004), Clinton described doing a Cleveland television interview "in which a man said he no longer supported me because I was spending all my time on gays in the military and Bosnia.... When he asked how much time I'd spent on gays in the military, and I told him just a few hours, he simply replied, 'I don't believe you.'"

General Colin Powell, chairman of the Joint Chiefs of Staff, called the president's proposal "prejudicial to good order and discipline." Powell was supported by the chief of naval operations, the army chief, and the commandant of the Marine Corps, who, according to Clinton's memoir, "made it clear that if I ordered them to take action they'd do the best they could, although if called to testify before Congress they would have to state their views frankly."

Senator Sam Nunn (D-Ga.), chairman of the Armed Services Committee and the leading expert on the military in the Senate, force-

"All right, men . . . as you were"
Cartoon by Kevin "KAL" Kallaugher, *Baltimore Sun* (www.kaltoons.com)

fully challenged Clinton. He was joined, in a moment of rare bipartisanship, by Senate minority leader Bob Dole (R-Kans.). The House of Representatives opposed Clinton by more than three to one.

A public opinion poll showed that lifting the ban was strongly approved by 16 percent of the electorate and strongly disapproved by 33 percent. Clinton noted, "It's hard to get politicians in swing districts to take a 17 percent deficit on any issue into an election." Activists confronted each other in Lafayette Park, across Pennsylvania Avenue from the White House, as they did in demonstrations and counterdemonstrations in Los Angeles, Seattle, Colorado Springs, and other cities.

Experienced presidents invent techniques to defuse potentially explosive issues—appoint a blue-ribbon commission, and set a deadline for action in the future. This is what General Powell had recommended in December 1992. Six months later, Clinton accepted a defense department proposal to create the "don't ask, don't tell" policy. But not before, in the opinion of transition scholars, he had hit the ground stumbling.

Presidential Commissions

Creating presidential commissions involves choosing a distinguished chairperson and a representative panel and setting a deadline for future action. These presidents also used them to cool hot issues.

President Kennedy: Commission on the Status of Women, 1961
Chaired by former First Lady Eleanor Roosevelt

President Nixon: Commission on Campus Unrest, 1970
Chaired by William Scranton, former governor of Pennsylvania

President Ford: Commission on CIA Activities within the United States, 1975
Chaired by Vice President Nelson Rockefeller

President Reagan: National Commission on Social Security Reform, 1983
Chaired by Alan Greenspan, former chairman of President Ford's Council of Economic Advisers

"It's time we end foreign oil dependence!"
Cartoon by Jimmy Margulies, ©2006, *The Record,* New Jersey

Extract from a Transition Memorandum

Early in 1980, Republican National Chairman Bill Brock invited me to serve on a task force he created to prepare material to be presented to the party's presidential nominee immediately after the national convention. My assignment was to help the candidate think about transition planning.

The next two chapters in this book will help you think about these questions as you begin assembling your White House staff and cabinet.

```
MEMO TO:    THE PARTY'S NOMINEE
FROM:       STEPHEN HESS
SUBJECT:    TRANSITION PLANNING
DATE:       MAY 22, 1980
```

. . . In a sense, you are immediately faced with three-dimensional decision-making: there are people decisions, structure decisions, and policy decisions. If you decide first on a person, you may become locked into a structure and/or a policy. Presidents-elect always make people decisions first, then rue many of the consequences. . . .

Assuming that you will want to get on with appointments, as have your predecessors, are there not ways to group together the consideration of certain jobs so as to keep policy and structure in mind at the same time? For example, by concentrating first on the triangle of State-Defense-NSC [National Security Council]? This mode of arranging your decisions can help you think about what you want of each agency and what qualities you most desire in a secretary of state, a secretary of defense, and a national security assistant. The same principle would apply to thinking about key economics positions.

Other factors enter into the appointing process: Do you want to give your cabinet officers the authority to choose their own deputy/under/assistant secretaries? Are there any jobs that can be best filled by setting up search committees? How much conflict/consensus do you wish to build into your advisory system? What sort of commitments do you want to get from your appointees? When you do not have specific people in mind, what are the most useful questions to ask candidates for each top job? What positions do you wish to abolish? What precedents need to be considered, such as a western governor for secretary of the interior? What part do you want members of Congress and the National Committee to play in people decisions? How do you want to go about screening candidates for conflicts of interest and other disqualifying characteristics? There needs to be a strategy for the announcement of appointments.

THE WHITE HOUSE

The White House is the obvious place to start putting the pieces in place that will define your administration. How do you wish to organize your staff? In what order should you make the appointments? Consider the degree of tension that you want to build into your system. What are the qualities you need in your key assistants? You will even have to give thought to the assignment of offices: who will be located near you in the West Wing and who will be across the street in the Eisenhower Executive Office Building? Who will help you face the press? As you make these and other decisions, the nation and the world will be assessing the rightness of your first moves.

CHAPTER 2

The White House

Staffing the White House

In the days before you become president of the United States (or POTUS, as we say "inside the Beltway"), the government may look like rows of empty offices waiting to be filled with your loyal supporters. This is not quite the case. Of the two million civilian employees in the U.S. government, you will get to pick about 3,000 of them. Moreover, the most important appointees will require confirmation by the U.S. Senate.

Let's get started at the top.

The White House Office

The nerve center of the Executive Office of the President is the White House Office (WHO). It is imperative to choose certain White House officials immediately in order to move forward efficiently with the staffing process—from selection to confirmation—that shapes your administration. Many problems of the Clinton transition arose because the president-elect—consumed, as he stated in his memoirs, with "micromanaging the cabinet appointments"—failed to appoint his White House staff, except for Chief of Staff Thomas F. McLarty, until six days before taking office.

The key positions that you must quickly fill are

- Chief of staff
- Personnel director
- Counsel
- Press secretary
- Congressional relations chief
- Speechwriters

Presidents usually designate one assistant their primus inter pares (Latin for "first among equals"), the PIP, in our shorthand. The PIP most often has the title "chief of staff"—but not always. Sherman Adams in the Eisenhower administration was "the assistant to the president" (with emphasis on "the"), and President Kennedy's PIP, Ted Sorensen, was "special counsel." Presidents Ronald Reagan and George W. Bush have had what amounted to multi-person PIPs. But titles and numbers matter much less than the PIP's dual responsibility to keep the president's policies moving forward while trying to keep him out of trouble. The PIP is the one job you will hopefully have picked—but not announced to the press—before the election. If you have not settled on your PIP yet, flip ahead in this chapter to the section "Picking Your PIP."

Quickly choosing the director of the Office of Presidential Personnel is especially important because of the heavy load of initial selections that must be made in the subcabinet: deputy secretaries, under secretaries, and assistant secretaries. Presidents once let cabinet members choose their own team, but you will undoubtedly agree with presidents since Ronald Reagan that it is best to retain this level of departmental control at the White House.

The White House counsel is "your lawyer." (The attorneys at the Justice Department are "the government's lawyers.") You are eventually going to need your lawyer for many questions relating to ethics, judicial selections, and delicate matters of using presidential powers. But right now you need the counsel to vet the appointees that are coming from the Personnel Office: by checking FBI full-field investigation reports, tax returns, searching for conflicts of interest.

The Cabinet

The core of the president's cabinet comprises the secretaries who head the fifteen government departments. Listed in the order in which they would succeed the president, they are the secretaries of State, Treasury, Defense, and the attorney general, and the secretaries of Interior, Agriculture, Commerce, Labor, Health and Human Services (HHS), Housing and Urban Development (HUD), Transportation, Energy, Education, Veterans Affairs, and Homeland Security.

There will be others to whom you award cabinet rank. Most recent presidents have put their chief of staff and the director of the Office of Management and Budget in their cabinets. Dwight Eisenhower put the UN ambassador in his cabinet, Ronald Reagan the director of the Central Intelligence Agency (CIA), Bill Clinton the head of the Small Business Administration (SBA), and George W. Bush the administrator of the Environmental Protection Agency (EPA). You may make similar decisions on the basis of how important you view these jobs to be. More often it is because of what you consider sufficient political reasons, such as to give a consolation prize to someone who really wants to be secretary of state or to add another demographic characteristic to your cabinet.

You may also want to keep some officials of the outgoing administration, either because they are good at their jobs or because it is too costly politically to replace them. The young John Kennedy was particularly skillful in this regard, providing instant reassurance by quickly reappointing J. Edgar Hoover as director of the Federal Bureau of Investigation (FBI) and Allen Dulles as CIA director.

The line of succession to the Office of President was established by the Presidential Succession Act of 1947. The law has been revised many times since 1947 to accommodate the creation of new departments, most recently in 2006 to add the Homeland Security secretary. Be sure your cabinet understands that the line of succession goes through the vice president, the Speaker of the House, and the president pro tempore of the Senate before arriving at the secretary of state.

Also remember this: the line of succession passed over Henry Kissinger, President Nixon's secretary of state, and Madeleine Albright, President Clinton's secretary of state, because they were both born outside of the United States to noncitizens, making them constitutionally ineligible to become president.

Organizing the White House Office

The White House Office is the one place in the government where you can mold the shape, size, and units to meet your specific needs. The WHO can take three basic shapes: circle, pyramid, or isosceles trapezoid (the isosceles trapezoid, as you may recall from your high school geometry, is a pyramid with the top cut off).

The circle with you in the center is usually called "the spokes in the wheel" design. It is most closely identified with Franklin Roosevelt and worked well when the president's staff was so small that they could all gather around his desk in the Oval Office. Presidents Ford and Carter tried it, but soon realized that without a chief of staff the president became his own chief of staff. (It is said that Carter's own staff work even included approving who could use the White House tennis court.)

The pyramid is principally identified with President Eisenhower who, after a lifetime in the military, knew how to make a steeply hierarchical system, with a chief of staff at its top, work for him. If you have not had experience with a large staff (U.S. senators and governors of small states fall into this category), this configuration may take some time getting used to. The pyramid promotes orderliness, but it may also screen out creativity.

The isosceles-trapezoid design permits more than one PIP. When President Reagan took office, his White House was run by the troika of James Baker as chief of staff, Edwin Meese overseeing policy development, and Michael Deaver in charge of the president's schedule, travel, and public image. President George W. Bush had a triple PIP in Andrew Card as chief of staff; Karen Hughes in charge of the offices of communications, press secretary, and speechwriting; and Karl Rove overseeing political affairs, intergovernmental affairs, and public liaison.

Once you have picked the best design to meet your management style, you can move on to staff selection. Most presidents arrange their White House Office into fifteen basic units, plus the chief of staff's office. But you will find several additional boxes on the White House organizational chart that you can reserve for special needs or new initiatives, such as President Clinton's Office for Women's Initiatives and Outreach and President George W. Bush's Office of Faith-Based and Community Initiatives.

The simplest organizational structure for your presidency is the circle. Guess who's in the center?

You

The chief of staff is alone at the top of the pyramid organization. It will help if you have had experience in running such a hierarchical **organization in the past.**

With this type of organizational structure, which looks like an isosceles trapezoid, your chief of staff will have some company at the top. Ideas and information may flow more freely to you from the people at the bottom.

The White House Office Organizational Chart

```
                    ┌──────────────┐
                    │    POTUS     │
                    └──────────────┘

┌─────────────────────────────────────────────────────────┐
│                    Chief of Staff                        │
└─────────────────────────────────────────────────────────┘
```

National Security Assistant	Economic Policy Assistant	Domestic Policy Assistant	Press Secretary

Cabinet Secretary[1]	Staff Secretary[2]	Management[3]

Personnel	Legal Counsel[4]	Speechwriters

Intergovernmental Affairs[5]	Congressional Relations

Communications[6]	Public Liaison[7]	Political Affairs[8]

For POTUS to add units

In the following boxes, fill in the names of other offices you want to make part of the White House Office:

1 Coordinates cabinet activities, including meetings, the weekly Cabinet Report, and other events.
2 The ultimate filter before a decision reaches the desk of the president, ensuring that all appropriate offices have coordinated and condensed the necessary information.
3 Manages all personnel, including the Military Office, and keeps all White House finances within budget.
4 Represents the president's legal interests and protects the constitutional prerogatives of the presidential office for the long term.
5 Facilitates cooperation and policy initiatives between the federal government and state, local, and tribal governments of the nation.
6 Coordinates the Public Affairs Offices of the executive branch to promote the president's policies.
7 Facilitates and maintains a working relationship with business and interest groups.
8 Maintains and improves the status of the president's party and its allies.

There are people who are loyal to you, who have spent years trying to get you elected, and who now want jobs in the government you are creating. It would be helpful if these people were already experienced in the executive branch. But, as you know, this is seldom so. What to do?

There will be *some* complementarity between campaign staff and White House staff, but only in spots—and it's dangerous to use the White House as a dumping ground. There is a history of loyalists getting the president in trouble.

All presidents bring with them a group of loyalists from their home states that come to be known by some epithet such as "the Irish Mafia" or "the Texas Rangers." President Carter followed this practice in the extreme: of the top eight White House positions, he gave seven to fellow Georgians. And of the seven, only one (domestic policy adviser Stuart Eizenstat) had previous experience in Washington.

Transition expert John P. Burke found that Carter "quite consciously and deliberately" valued loyalty over Washington experience. Carter said what he most needed were aides "who were compatible with each other and who were loyal to me." Unfortunately, this staff was not well designed for getting the president's program through Congress. Even before Carter formally took office, Tip O'Neill, the new Speaker of the House and a fellow Democrat, told Hamilton Jordan, Carter's top assistant, "I'll ream your ass before I'm through." These were crude—but prophetic—words.

As Charles O. Jones, Neustadt's worthy successor among presidential transition scholars, recommends, "If the president-elect and his aides are not Washington-wise, then they are advised to get help." Those leaving government are usually eager to explain the ropes to the newcomers, regardless of party, even when "my" president was just defeated by "your" president. Example: On November 20, 1976, in the month that Carter defeated Gerald Ford, I went to the White House, representing President-elect Carter, to meet with President Ford's chief of staff, Dick Cheney. For two and a half hours on a quiet Saturday morning, Cheney laid out the White House manning charts, unit by unit, suggesting changes. By the time we finished, I was able to send Carter a memo proposing a seventy-seven person staff reduction.

Moreover, by the time incomers become outgoers they will have learned how much talent resides in the upper reaches of the permanent government—those unloved bureaucrats. They are there to be useful on arrival—if asked. Example: When Pat Moynihan wanted to educate the young staff of the newly created White House Council on Urban Affairs in 1969, he called in a Bureau of the Budget examiner to give morning tutorials. The talented bureaucrat was Paul O'Neill, who will later enter this story in another capacity.

Lessons to Apply to Your Transition

☞ *When hiring political loyalists, make sure they have the right skills for the job. Never forget "Brownie, you're doing a heck of a job"—the response of President George W. Bush to Michael Brown during a September 2, 2005, briefing on the Hurricane Katrina disaster. Brown was forced out of his job as director of the Federal Emergency Management Agency ten days later. His job before joining the Bush administration? Judges and stewards commissioner for the International Arabian Horse Association.*

☞ *Tell your appointees that you expect them to schedule serious conversations (not mere courtesy calls) with their departing counterparts.*

☞ *Incoming officials should ask their outgoing counterparts to permit top civil servants to give them the type of information they would like to have had when they first got their jobs.*

Location, Location, Location

There are more glorious offices for your staff than those in the West Wing. The TV show of that name did not depict how small and even windowless some of the latter really are. Just across the gated West Executive Street stands another building whose rooms have mile-high ceilings, elegant moldings, historic door handles. This is the Eisenhower Executive Office Building, which once housed the State, War, and Navy Departments. Nevertheless, all of your advisers and staff will want to be crammed together in the West Wing—because that is where the Oval Office is. Some of your staff may not accept space elsewhere without a struggle.

The struggle for space in the West Wing is neatly illustrated by a transition story that Madeleine Albright tells in her book *Memo to the President Elect* (HarperCollins, 2008). She was on President Carter's National Security Council staff, "which was run by [Zbigniew] Brzezinski from a large corner office in the White House West Wing. I had the duty of personally escorting Reagan's first national security advisor, Richard Allen, past a warren of cubbyholes and clutter to the tiny basement office that he had been assigned by the Reagan team. Allen's face fell a foot." Allen lasted only a year, and his successor managed to get himself back into a first-floor corner office.

The West Wing on TV

For those of us who have had offices in the real West Wing (mine was on the ground floor), the set of the television show that ran on NBC from 1999 to 2006 was much more accurate than many other recreations in movies and television—and yet it was still full of inaccuracies. You could say it was true in spirit but had been adjusted to make room for the right camera angles. For example, the large open office area doesn't exist. The beautiful lobby seen on television is much smaller in the real West Wing. TV's Roosevelt Room is entirely a creation of producer Aaron Sorkin—there are no burgundy walls and French doors. Strangely, the TV version has no Cabinet Room, which is replaced by something called the Mural Room. What I usually tell people who ask for a comparison is that the real West Wing is a very quiet place—as though the staff were saying to each other, "Shh! The president is working." At least in the presidencies I've known there was not a lot of shouting and running down the halls of the West Wing.

You can find some very good information on the features of the West Wing in Pete Sharkey's website, www.whitehousemuseum.org. This is a private website that is not affiliated with the White House Historical Association or the U.S. government.

Down the hall from the Oval Office, the other large first-floor corner office belongs to the chief of staff (see the West Wing Floor Plan on page 22). The press secretary also rates an excellent first-floor office because of the necessity of being close to the briefing room and the nattering nabobs of the media.

The first lady, with her staff, is usually in the East Wing, on the other side of the Residence (known as the Mansion in earlier days). But one recent first lady, Hillary Rodham Clinton, had her own office in the West Wing—although it was not an especially grand one. Another new development: recent vice presidents have also staked out space in the West Wing, although their "grand" office is in the Capitol by virtue of the vice president's role as presiding officer of the Senate.

Beyond these top-tier officials, there is room for competition.

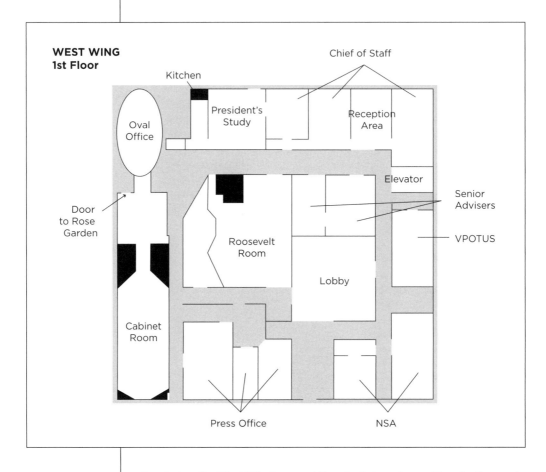

WEST WING
1st Floor

Chief of Staff

Kitchen

Oval Office

President's Study

Reception Area

Door to Rose Garden

Elevator

Senior Advisers

VPOTUS

Roosevelt Room

Lobby

Cabinet Room

Press Office

NSA

Located on the West Wing's ground floor (not shown) are offices for the president's schedulers and security staff, staff secretary, the White House photographer, video-teleconferencing room (the "situation room"), the staff mess, and a small conference room.

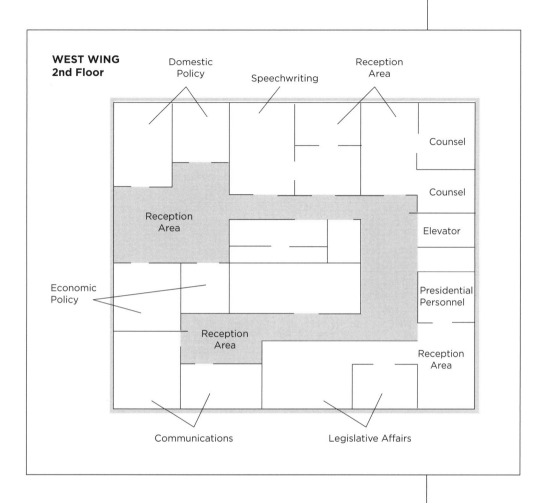

WEST WING 2nd Floor

Domestic Policy

Speechwriting

Reception Area

Counsel

Counsel

Reception Area

Elevator

Economic Policy

Presidential Personnel

Reception Area

Reception Area

Communications

Legislative Affairs

Pick a Presidential Portrait

George Washington by Gilbert Stuart (1775–1828)
Hung in the Oval Office during the presidencies of Lyndon Johnson and Richard Nixon.

The Eisenhower Executive Office Building

The Eisenhower Executive Office Building (EEOB) fills an entire city block west of the White House. It is home for some of the overflow from the West Wing, which is just across a gated street, West Executive Avenue. Originally built in the late nineteenth century to house the entire State Department, War Department, and Navy Department, the building contained (when I worked there in 1959 and 1960) a half floor of White House aides plus the National Security Council staff, the Bureau of the Budget, the Office of Civil and Defense Mobilization, and the Council of Economic Advisers.

Architecturally, EEOB is described as French Second Empire in design, but also as "General Grant Renaissance," an awkward collection of extended porches, sharp dormers, mansard roofs, hundreds of small columns, tall chimneys, four-feet-thick outside walls, and granite stairways so constructed that should one step give way, five floors of steps would come tumbling down. Part of my affection for the building is that it is so ugly. The story goes that Calvin Coolidge was given a tour and asked only one question: "Is it insured against fire and earthquake?" "Of course, Mr. President," answered his guide. "What a pity," replied Coolidge. (The story is apocryphal; government buildings are not insured.)

But what I love most, of course, was having had an office there. I was twenty-five years old. In Room 276 I had doorknobs of brass emblazoned with the seal of the War Department and long iron pipes fastened high on the walls, which once held the regimental banners of defeated armies. When I had meetings at my long conference table, I made sure a White House notepad lay at each place so that my conferees could steal them. From my windows I watched important people avoid the press by entering the West Wing through the side door or the president's helicopter land on the orange stripes that had been placed on the South Lawn—the president holding tight to his fedora as he disembarked under the windy whirl of the chopper's blades—or could see the red and white candy-striped canopies sheltering Mrs. Eisenhower's lawn party.

Lessons to Apply to Your Transition

☞ *Make sure your PIP reviews office assignments with you before showing them to anyone else. Adjustments may be necessary.*

☞ *The basic rule for assigning West Wing offices is simple and straightforward: the more you need to see someone, the closer his or her office should be to the Oval Office.*

Picking Your PIP

What skills make for the perfect primus inter pares, first among equals? Certainly not those of the campaign manager, although some campaign managers may have PIP skills. James Carville knew his talents were in campaigning, not governing, and rightly chose to stay out of the Clinton White House. President Carter's campaign manager, Hamilton Jordan, was never at ease with the ways Washington does business and should have resisted more strenuously the PIP job in which he was such a bad fit.

The PIP should be deeply schooled in and sensitive to the arcane ways of Washington. President Reagan chose insider James Baker as his chief of staff, a selection that gave the president the luxury of adding two California associates who lacked Washington experience to complete his three-person PIP. President George W. Bush achieved a similar arrangement by combining Washington insider Andrew Card with two Texans, Karen Hughes and Karl Rove, to create his initial PIP.

The PIP is your fail-safe mechanism, the last redoubt between you and a misstep. If the PIP does not know the location of all the traps that will be set for you in the capital, you are likely to get ensnared. This ability should be the key qualification of the PIP; the rest—the public relations skills or policy development skills—can be brought into the White House in subordinate positions, if necessary.

Donald Regan described his PIP role in the Reagan White House as leading the "shovel brigade that follows [the] parade down Main Street." But in a job as inherently overbearing as that of the PIP, nuance as a management tool can go a long way. Heavy-handed managers such as Regan, Haldeman (Nixon), and John Sununu (George H. W. Bush)—

The President's Initial Primus inter Pares

President and PIP/title	Age	Prior position(s)	Circumstances of exit
Dwight D. Eisenhower (1953–61)			
Sherman Adams, assistant to the president (1953–58)	54	Governor of New Hampshire (1949–53)	Vicuña scandal*
John F. Kennedy (1961–63)			
Ted Sorensen, special counsel (1961–63)	33	Aide to Senator John F. Kennedy (1953–61)	Death of President Kennedy
Richard M. Nixon (1969–74)			
H. R. Haldeman, chief of staff (1969–73)	43	Campaign manager (1962, 1968)	Watergate scandal**
Jimmy Carter (1977–81)			
Hamilton Jordan, chief adviser (1977–79), chief of staff (1979–80)	33	Campaign manager (1970, 1976)	Carter's defeat in 1980
Ronald Reagan (1981–88)			
James A. Baker, chief of staff (1981–85)	50	Campaign manager: Ford (1976), George H. W. Bush (1980)	Became secretary of treasury
Edwin Meese III, counselor to the president (1981–85)	49	Governor Reagan's chief of staff (1969–74)	Became attorney general
Michael Deaver, deputy chief of staff (1981–85)	43	Governor Reagan's deputy chief of staff (1969–74)	Resigned
George H. W. Bush (1989–93)			
John H. Sununu, chief of staff (1989–91)	49	Governor of New Hampshire (1983–89)	Air Sununu scandal***
Bill Clinton (1993–2001)			
Thomas F. "Mack" McLarty III, chief of staff (1993–94)	47	CEO of Arkla, Inc. (1985–93)	Became counselor to President Clinton for trade issues
George W. Bush (2001–09)			
Andrew Card, chief of staff (2001–06)	54	Secretary of transportation (1992–93)	Resigned
Karl Rove, senior adviser (2001–07)	50	Campaign consultant for Bush (1994, 1998, 2000, 2004)	Resigned
Karen Hughes, counselor to the president (2001–02)	45	Governor Bush's director of communications (1995–2000)	Became under secretary of state for public diplomacy (2005)

* Adams was pressured to resign after reports surfaced that he had accepted an expensive vicuña overcoat and other favors from a Boston textile manufacturer being investigated for Federal Trade Commission violations.

** On January 1, 1975, Haldeman was convicted of conspiracy and obstruction of justice and sentenced to an eighteen-month prison sentence for his role in the Watergate scandal.

*** Sununu resigned after reports revealed that he had used military aircraft for personal trips costing upward of $615,000.

who interpreted their responsibilities largely in managerial terms—have tended to serve their presidents least well. They made enemies faster and said "no" more often. In the case of Regan, he made enemies—he clashed frequently with First Lady Nancy Reagan, who, he wrote in his memoirs, used her personal astrologer to help schedule the president's speaking engagements—but still was not able to keep President Reagan from being implicated in the arms for hostages swap with Iran.

So what background offers the greatest possibility for success? Howard Baker was unique in that he was pressed into service, in 1987, to add his own prestige as the former Senate majority leader to the battered Reagan presidency in the wake of the Iran-Contra scandal. Other PIPs had briefer service as House members, as in the case of Sherman Adams (Eisenhower), Donald Rumsfeld (Ford), and Leon Panetta (Clinton), or as congressional staffers, as with Ted Sorensen (Kennedy), Walter Jenkins (Lyndon Johnson), and Kenneth Duberstein (Reagan).

An understanding of the legislature is helpful—but ignorance of Congress is fatal.

Worksheet

Four Questions for Your PIP

Before settling on a PIP, you may wish to ask your top candidates the following questions:

1. Are you capable of firing my closest friend because I can't look him in the eyes?
   ❏ Yes   ❏ Not sure

2. When on "Meet the Press," will you enthusiastically support a policy of mine that I know you detest?
   ❏ Yes   ❏ Not sure

3. Can you take the blame for "forgetting" to invite a major contributor to the state dinner for the Queen of England?
   ❏ Yes   ❏ Not sure

4. Will you set an example for the White House staff by working longer hours and seeing less of your family?
   ❏ Yes   ❏ Not sure

If the answer to each of these questions is yes, you may have found yourself the perfect PIP.

As you are about to be surrounded by strangers, supplicants, and sycophants, you may be tempted to turn to a familiar face, a trusted friend, to fill the role of your PIP. Try to resist. The record is not promising—as the sad experience of President Bill Clinton and his best friend, Chief of Staff Thomas "Mack" McLarty, illustrates vividly.

They were together in Miss Mary's kindergarten class in Hope, Arkansas. Mack was two months older than Bill. Mack's family stayed in Hope, Bill's family moved to Hot Springs. They stayed in touch. When Bill successfully ran for governor in 1978, Mack was his treasurer. Mack was successful in his own right: first as a member of the Arkansas legislature and later as chairman and chief executive officer of Arkla, a Fortune 500 natural gas company.

So when Bill Clinton was elected president of the United States he asked Mack McLarty, his "loyal friend of more than forty years," to become his chief of staff. As Clinton recalled in his memoirs, "It was an unusual choice because . . . he was hardly a Washington insider, a fact that concerned him. He told me he would prefer another job more suited to his business background. Nevertheless, I pressed Mack to accept the position."

Mack's problems in running a tight ship at the White House might have been obvious from the beginning. His appointment was not announced until December 12, and it took more than a month for Clinton to fill the other White House positions: the slowest start in transition history. There would be no staff learning time before the inauguration. Clinton's party had lost the last three presidential elections, so there were few Democrats knowledgeable in White House management waiting to be hired. And because dark-horse candidates for presidential nominations like Clinton do not get the pick of experienced campaign workers, the staff McLarty was to lead seemed destined to be filled with young enthusiasts.

Nor do new presidents quickly change their ways. Possibly the worst place for presidential job training is a small one-party state where it is possible for a smart and energetic chief executive to know everyone and everything, be everywhere, and succeed. When transferred to Washington, Clinton continued to run late and hold meetings that were seemingly unending.

McLarty found the pace at the White House to be different from what he had mastered in the private sector: many more issues, many more decisions, coming at him faster, in a less deliberate process. But the Washington scene and relations with journalists did not rattle him as they had the Georgians who arrived with Carter. His collegial demeanor earned him the nickname "Mack the Nice."

The president had an exceptionally painful first year: gays in the military, successive nominations of attorneys general, a deadly raid on the Branch Davidian cult in Waco, Texas, a scandal over the firing of White House Travel Office employees. Could McLarty have eased the president's burdens? Clinton apparently thought so. His memoir suggests that his problems resulted in part from the two of them ("he and I") suffering "from some of our tone deafness about Washington's political and press culture."

But Robert Reich, from his observation post in Clinton's cabinet as secretary of labor, chose to identify causes beyond a lack of Washington experience. "Poor Mack," Reich wrote in *Locked in the Cabinet* (Vintage, 1997), a memoir of his four years in the Clinton administration, "has been unable to impose discipline on a chronically undisciplined president and a chaotic White House staff."

On June 28, 1993, seventeen months into his term, Clinton replaced McLarty as chief of staff with Leon Panetta, his director of the Office of Management and Budget, who had had a long career in Congress. Panetta immediately tightened White House operations. Staff work and decision memoranda to the president would henceforth go through him. He took control of staff payroll and hiring. The size of senior staff meetings was cut from thirty to ten, and direct staff access to the Oval Office went from ten to two. Perhaps Panetta could not have created this order if he had been Clinton's first chief of staff rather than his second.

McLarty, however, did not go home. He stayed at the White House for five years after exiting the chief of staff's suite, moving to a West Wing ground floor office from which he helped his presidential friend secure international financing for peacekeeping operations in Bosnia, win congressional approval of the North American Free Trade Agreement (NAFTA), structure the 1995 Mexican peso stabilization program, and organize two hemispheric summit meetings as Clinton's "special envoy to the Americas." Many Latin American countries awarded him their highest civilian honors. Since 1999 he has been president of McLarty Associates (formerly Kissinger McLarty Associates), an international strategic advisory and advocacy firm.

Picking Your Press Secretary

It would be useful if your press secretary had great briefing skills: an ability to explain your policies with brevity and accuracy, to deflect difficult questions without rancor, and to cut tension with good humor or a quip. It would also be useful if reporters considered your press secretary to be a fun sort of person—if only because they will have to spend so much time together and because nothing is gained by a hostile workplace.

It would be useful, but not sufficient.

Pierre Salinger, President Kennedy's press secretary, had all these skills. He was a good fellow, but the White House press corps at the time did not hold him in the highest regard. Why? Because he lacked what reporters consider the one essential: membership in the president's inner circle. When important decisions were being debated in the White House about the Bay of Pigs invasion, Salinger's name was not on the manifest. The opposite was true of President Carter's press secretary, Jody Powell. Powell was far from a personal favorite of the Washington press corps, yet he was valued for his closeness to Carter.

News organizations spend a lot of money to cover you, yet White House reporters will have limited opportunities to ask you questions directly (unless you are very different from those who came before you). Because of this, reporters need to feel the information they get from your press secretary is bankable.

So, what career path produces the perfect press secretary—journalism or political communications? Ideally, your

"I have a brief statement, a clarification, and two denials."

Cartoon by Peter Steiner, ©The New Yorker

press secretary will have a background in both fields. This was the case with President Eisenhower's press secretary, James Hagerty, who invented the modern White House Press Office. Hagerty had been a reporter for the *New York Times* before becoming press secretary to New York Governor Thomas Dewey and, later, the spokesman for Ike's 1952 presidential campaign.

Rating Press Secretaries

The first presidential assistant whose sole responsibility was press relations—hence the first press secretary—was George Akerson, who served (not very successfully) from 1929 to 1931 under Herbert Hoover. Through the George W. Bush presidency, twenty-seven men and two women have held the job. Here are my picks for the top three:

1. James C. Hagerty (Eisenhower, 1953–61)
Jim Hagerty earns my top rating if only for a month of briefings in the fall of 1955. On September 23, while vacationing in Denver, Eisenhower had a serious heart attack. For three weeks Hagerty held five briefings a day, releasing such intimate details as the number of bowel movements recorded on the president's medical chart. The illnesses of previous presidents, most notably Woodrow Wilson, had been shrouded in mystery and lies. Hagerty's full frankness policy (obviously with Eisenhower's support) reversed the way the White House now responds to presidential illnesses.

2. Marlin Fitzwater (Reagan, 1987–89; George H. W. Bush, 1989–93)
Except for short carryover periods during unexpected changes in presidential administrations, press secretaries serve one president. What elevates the genial Marlin Fitzwater to the top of the pantheon of press secretaries is that he was so skillful in representing two presidents of such different personalities, abilities, and needs.

3. Mike McCurry (Clinton, 1994–98)
Measure the degree of a president's hostility to the press, measure the degree of the press corps' suspicion of a president's truthfulness, then put a press secretary in the crosshairs where they meet and you describe Mike McCurry at the White House during the Monica Lewinsky scandal. I doubt any press secretary could have done a better job of trying to direct reporters to everything else in the nation and the world that the Clinton presidency was engaged in.

But if your press secretary doesn't have experience in both careers, the record suggests a background as a political communicator is the better fit. The estimable James Brady came to the Reagan press operation after having handled press relations for the OMB in the Ford administration and having been chief spokesman for a defense secretary and a senator.

The fundamental duality of the White House job is less wearing on the political communicator. As Hagerty told reporters, "I'm here to help you get the news. I am also here to work for one man, who happens to be the President. And I will do that to the best of my ability."

Press secretaries who come to the White House with a journalism-only background seem more conflicted. Jerald terHorst, who left the Washington bureau of the *Detroit News* to become President Ford's first press secretary, lasted only thirty days, resigning when he could not support Ford's decision to pardon former President Nixon. TerHorst was an honorable man who made a conscientious decision—but it was not a decision that was helpful to President Ford.

The usual habit is to elevate the campaign spokesman. In some recent cases, unfortunately, this has not produced complete satisfaction.

Press Secretaries on Press Secretaries

Joe Lockhart (Clinton, 1997–2000)

If you had asked me before I was going out to my daily briefing—if you'd given me the choice [of] five minutes with the president or . . . five minutes with John Podesta, the chief of staff, most days I'd take it with the chief of staff. Because in the structure of the White House that I worked in, that was where all roads led to. I could, in three or four minutes, find out what was going on throughout the government—all the things that were likely. Whereas half of these decisions hadn't made it to the president's desk yet.

Ron Nessen (Ford, 1974–77)

People in the White House never trust the press secretary. It's one of the reasons why the single most important quality for a good press secretary is access. To get the information firsthand, so you don't have to ask somebody how should I answer this question. That is the most important quality. And I think there's this sense among other White House staff people, "Gee, if we don't tell the press secretary, he won't accidentally blurt it out when we don't want anybody to know about it, or not right now, anyway."

Source: Stephen Hess and Marvin Kalb, editors, *The Media and the War on Terrorism* (Brookings, 2003).

Lesson to Apply to Your Transition

☞ *Ask candidates for press secretary to repeat after you this "oath" of office:*

"I, _____ , am here to work for the President and it is my job to explain my president's position—whatever it is—to the best of my ability."

Messages

There is nothing you can do during your transition that will not be interpreted and reinterpreted by careful—and careless—observers. You can limit confusion by making your announcements as explicit as possible, or by running them in sequences (what's first, what's second?), or by bundling (what messages go together?). Unfortunately, most presidents-in-transition simply announce their intentions as they make up their minds and thus fail to take advantage of the early opportunities. If you don't tell us what you mean, others will.

Action	Reaction
Eisenhower puts the UN ambassador in the cabinet.	Is this a policy change or simply payback to Lodge?
Kennedy retains Hoover as FBI director and Allen Dulles at the CIA.	Keep watching "the hidden hand" of old Joe Kennedy.
Nixon appoints Harvard professors Kissinger and Moynihan to his White House staff.	Maybe Herblock's right and a "new Nixon" deserves a "free shave."
Seven of Carter's top eight White House aides are from Georgia.	Maybe he doesn't trust anybody else.
James Baker becomes Reagan's chief of staff.	Did you know Reagan is that cunning? What does this mean for Meese?
Bush retains three of Reagan's cabinet.	Count on bloodletting between the holdovers and the Bush people who want in.
Clinton assigns health care to Hillary.	"Buy one; get one free."
Cheney is the voice of the transition.	Who's in change over there, anyway?

Lessons to Apply to Your Transition

☞ *Decide on the impression you want to make with these early announcements.*

☞ *Take advantage of the size of your initial audience; everyone's listening now.*

☞ *When do you prefer to have others deliver the message?*

☞ *Whom do you want to speak for you?*

Presidents and Their Initial Press Secretaries

	Age	Campaign experience
President Dwight D. Eisenhower (1953–61)		
James C. Hagerty (1953–61)	44	Eisenhower presidential campaign (1952)
President John F. Kennedy (1961–63)		
Pierre Salinger (1961–63)	36	Kennedy presidential campaign (1960)
President Richard M. Nixon (1969–74)		
Ron Ziegler (1969–74)	29	Nixon presidential campaign (1964), Nixon gubernatorial campaign (1962)
President Jimmy Carter (1977–81)		
Jody Powell (1977–81)	34	Carter presidential campaign (1976)
President Ronald Reagan (1981–88)		
James Brady (1981–87)	41	Reagan presidential campaign (1980)
Larry Speakes (1981–87)*	42	Reagan presidential campaign (1980)
President George H. W. Bush (1989–93)		
Marlin Fitzwater (1989–93)	47	Bush presidential campaign (1988)
President Bill Clinton (1993–2001)		
Dee Dee Myers (1993–94)	32	Presidential campaigns of Michael Dukakis (1988) and Bill Clinton (1992)
George Stephanopoulos (1993)**	32	Presidential campaigns of Michael Dukakis (1988) and Bill Clinton (1992)
George W. Bush (2001–09)		
Ari Fleischer (2000–03)	40	Presidential campaigns of George H. W. Bush (1992) and George W. Bush (2000)

* Brady was unable to return to work after being shot during the assassination attempt on President Reagan on March 30, 1981. Although Brady retained the title of Press Secretary, Larry Speakes performed those duties as Acting Press Secretary.

** Dee Dee Myers was the official Press Secretary. However, communications director George Stephanopoulos gave the press briefings during the first six months of the Clinton administration.

Journalism experience	Government experience
Reporter, *New York Times* (1934–42)	Press secretary for New York Governor Thomas E. Dewey (1943–52)
Reporter, *San Francisco Chronicle* and contributing editor, *Collier's* (1940s and 1950s)	Investigator with Robert Kennedy on the Senate anti-racketeering committee (1957–59)
None	None
None	Press secretary for Georgia Governor Jimmy Carter
None	Press secretary for various government departments (1973–77)
Journalist/editor for various Mississippi newspapers (1961–68)	Press secretary for Presidents Nixon and Ford (1974–77)
Journalist for various Kansas newspapers (1961–65)	Press secretary for Vice President Bush (1985–87), President Reagan (1987–89)
None	None
None	Aide to Representative Richard Gephardt (1988–92)
None	Press secretary for various Republicans (1982–94)

Picking Your Congressional Lobbyist

No job on your staff will have as large a pool of talented people to choose from. Draw a circle with a ten-mile radius from the White House, and you will capture dozens—if not hundreds—of members of your party who have vast experience as former members of Congress or as current or former congressional staffers. Most will take a substantial cut in pay to become your chief lobbyist. Why? Because the job is important, it is fun for the right kind of person, it is highly visible in their world of political advocacy—and it is only deferred income anyway.

What is amazing is that one president-elect could get this pick so wrong. Jimmy Carter chose a man without any Capitol Hill experience, whose lobbying history was limited to the Georgia legislature. Warned away from this selection during the transition, Carter adamantly replied, "Frank Moore is my man."

Within a month of taking office, Carter had proposed eliminating or reducing federal funds for eighteen water projects in sixteen states. To the legislators who had not been consulted, these were not wasteful pork-barrel projects. The Senate promptly passed an amendment requiring that the projects be built. This was Carter's "first decision," recalled budget director Bert Lance in his memoirs *The Truth of the Matter* (Summit Books, 1991), and it "alienated about as many members of Congress that you can possibly do." Carter's policy agenda created a serious legislative overload, with too many proposals going too quickly to the same committees at the same time. Speaker of the House Tip O'Neill concluded that Moore "didn't know beans about Congress."

Now consider an earlier presidential transition aided by a man whose career had included managing congressional relations for two presidents: Bryce N. Harlow, who in November 1968 was working at New York City's Hotel Pierre, headquarters for President-elect Nixon:

> I'm there in this room, phones ringing, jumping off the wall. Suddenly over runs a secretary, "Mr. Harlow, President Johnson's calling." I cut off who I was talking to and I said, "Yes, Mr. President . . . yuppity yup, yes, sir. . . ." And over runs the secretary. I put my hand over the receiver. "President Eisenhower is calling." "Tell him I'm talking to the President

Margins Matter

Statistically speaking, Frank Moore's job as President Jimmy Carter's chief congressional lobbyist should not have been as difficult as it later became when presidents faced closely divided Congresses. The Democrats in Carter's first Congress held significant margins over the Republicans in both chambers. Only the three Democratic presidents-elect—Kennedy, Carter, and Clinton—came into office with a majority in Senate and House. In 2001 Gorge W. Bush had an evenly split Senate—and hence the vice president could cast a deciding vote.

President and Congress	Senate		House	
	Democrats	Republicans	Democrats	Republicans
John F. Kennedy 87th Congress (1961–63)	64 (+28)	36	262 (+87)	175
Richard M. Nixon 91st Congress (1969–71)	58 (+16)	42	243 (+51)	192
Jimmy Carter 95th Congress (1977–79)	61 (+23)	38	292 (+149)	143
Ronald Reagan 97th Congress (1981–83)	46	53 (+7)	242 (+50)	192
George H. W. Bush 101st Congress (1989–91)	55 (+10)	45	260 (+85)	175
Bill Clinton 103rd Congress (1993–95)	57 (+14)	43	258 (+82)	176
George W. Bush 107th Congress (2001–03)	50	50	212	221 (+9)

and I'll call him right back, or if he prefers, we'll put him on hold." Believe me, we put President Eisenhower on hold. Now I've got the President [on the line], got the former President waiting. In runs [Nixon aide] Larry Higby, and he says, "Mr. Harlow, Mr. Harlow," very imperiously, "The President-elect wants you in his office immediately."

The story of a man whose counsel was demanded simultaneously by a former president, the current president, and the future president may suggest an extraordinary ego. But Harlow was a small, unassuming man who spoke almost in whispers and gladly let others take credit. His résumé: after graduating from the University of Oklahoma, Harlow went to Washington and became an assistant to his member of Congress. He rose to chief clerk of the House Armed Services Committee and was the Pentagon's liaison officer to Congress during World War II. He was the chief lobbyist for Presidents Eisenhower and Nixon and, between these periods of White House service, directed the governmental relations office of Proctor & Gamble. In other words, Harlow was a man who had worked long and hard to take the measure of government.

What made Harlow such an effective bridge between the executive and legislative branches was his skill as a negotiator. As the

Bryce Harlow—In His Own Words

The White House is the universe of American politics. It's where everything comes together and therefore should be the most universal place in the whole operation of the government. Oddly, it becomes the most parochial place because of the way the White House functions and because of the steel fences around the White House manned by police to keep people out. . . .

It's rather axiomatic in this work [White House lobbying] that a president cannot have too many congressional issues that are "presidential" at one time. Otherwise none of them are presidential, and all of them suffer. My rule of thumb is that a president should not have more than about five really presidential issues working at a time. There's no way to get the members of Congress to react to them as all presidential. Fewer if possible is better. . . .

All of us who have been around the process very long realize that politics is not a hobby, it's a business. The bottom line is not profit and loss, it's votes. A congressman's profit is more votes than a competitor can get. That puts him in the black. So whatever contributes to his getting a profit in the next election instead of a deficit, which is fatal, is a motivator for him. A lot of people sneer at this and say it creates only weathervane, thoughtless robots, but that's the way our system is. The members of the Congress are supposed to reflect the will of the people of the United States. So they do that.

Source: Bryce Harlow interview with the author, 1976.

go-between, he had an uncanny knack for discerning what was most crucial to each player. He knew when a legislator could afford to give in and when the legislator would have to stand firm. He understood the trick was to make sure, if possible, that everyone would be able to claim some victory. Moreover, he was eminently practical: his job was to solve problems for the president—not to turn legislative proposals into moral imperatives.

In seeking a Harlow type—and they're still around—you should make sure that they report each side accurately to the other, that they do not promise what they cannot deliver, that they do not make cutting comments in drawing rooms for recirculation in gossip columns and blogs, and that they do not call opponents' motives into question.

Lessons to Apply to Your Transition

☞ *Make sure you know that the person who will represent you has the trust of the congressional leadership of both parties.*

☞ *Require a "recusal" commitment: no contact with former clients on matters before Congress.*

☞ *Require a four-year commitment to discourage in-and-out opportunists.*

Picking Your Speechwriters

No president had a White House speechwriting shop as oddly constructed as Richard Nixon's. Its three senior writers were about as far apart in background and ideology as it is possible to get: Raymond Price (liberal, WASP), Patrick Buchanan (conservative, Catholic), and William Safire (centrist, Jew). According to Safire, "When Nixon wanted to take a shot at somebody, he turned to Buchanan. . . . When Nixon wanted a vision of the nation's future, he turned to Price." Safire himself contributed "a touch of humor." Nixon did not want them to work together as a committee. The moral of the story is, I guess, that a president can have any type of staff that he feels serves his purpose.

Pick a Presidential Portrait

George Washington by Charles Willson Peale (1741–1827)
*Hung in the Oval Office during the presidencies of Richard Nixon,
Gerald Ford, Jimmy Carter, and Ronald Reagan.*

Where you look for a speechwriter also defies a simple answer. Among those who did heavy work for Franklin Roosevelt, Raymond Moley was a professor at Columbia University, Samuel Rosenman left his seat on the New York Supreme Court to join the White House staff (not as a lawyer, but as the speechwriter), Robert Sherwood was a playwright who won four Pulitzer Prizes, Archibald MacLeish was a poet who won three Pulitzers, and Charles Michelson was the publicity chief at the Democratic National Committee. Good speechwriters are merely people who are good at putting words—in speech form—in other people's mouths.

Since you already have speechwriters—presidential candidates have to have them, as well as those who hold the jobs that lead to the presidency—your basic question is probably not where to find them but what you do with them in the White House. The argument among scholars revolves around whether to put them in their own box (and direct them to stay in it) or distribute them among policymaking offices, as they were in an earlier time.

The problem is that presidents now make so many more speeches. Robert Schlesinger, in *White House Ghosts: Presidents and Their Speechwriters* (Simon & Schuster, 2008), notes that Herbert Hoover averaged eight public appearances a month, Kennedy nearly nineteen, and Clinton more than twenty-eight. Your speechwriters will have to be tightly organized to meet this demand. At the same time, you should seek ways to take advantage of the talents they could bring to creating your policies, not just to explaining them.

Ghost Stories

In these days, when speechwriters are often better known than the people for whom they write speeches, it is hard to recall that they were once known as "ghosts." One of Franklin Roosevelt's writers—Charles Michelson—even called his memoirs *The Ghost Talks* (G. P. Putnam's Sons, 1944).

Gloomdoggle

My first words for Dwight D. Eisenhower were spoken on September 26, 1958, at the bicentennial celebration of Fort Ligonier, in Pennsylvania, which had just been restored: "Today we see it much as it must have appeared to young Colonel Washington two hundred years ago." I had been hired at age twenty-five to assist my college mentor, Malcolm Moos, in working primarily on the president's campaign speeches in what was to be a disastrous midterm congressional election. The country was in the midst of a deep recession, and my instructions were to keep calling the Democrats "prophets of gloom and doom," a phrase I truly detested by the end of October.

The president's last campaign speech was to be in Baltimore on October 31, and we were meeting in Dr. Moos's East Wing office to review my draft. The "we" was a team of staff lawyers there to nix anything that could not be sworn to in court. This would be a problem—for I had made up a word to replace "gloom and doom": gloomdoggle. If boondoggle means "create unneeded work," then surely gloomdoggle could mean "create unneeded gloom." The lawyers hated my invention. But Mac Moos's wife, Tracey, an effervescent lady, suddenly burst into the room, spread enthusiasm for keeping my word in the draft, and won the day. The president loved his new word—as he often did with the colorful phrases we sneaked past the vetters. (He had once been a speechwriter himself.)

So we trooped off to Baltimore to hear the president. When the cheering stopped and we left the Fifth Regiment Armory, newsboys were hawking the bulldog edition of the next day's *Baltimore Sun*. Across an eight-column front page, in all caps and the boldest, blackest, largest type short of declaring war, ran the headline:

IKE CALLS DEMOCRATS "GLOOMDOGGLERS"
IN SPEECH HERE CLOSING THE CAMPAIGN

The page—framed, of course—is the only bit of political memorabilia that I keep in my office.

Dinner with Ike

If ever there was a case of divine intervention on behalf of the harried speechwriter, it occurred just before a "Dinner with Ike" for 7,000 in Los Angeles on January 27, 1960. The speech of that evening was a big deal: eighty-three dinners around the country designed to raise $5 million were connected by closed-circuit TV, with Richard Nixon in Chicago, Nelson Rockefeller in Washington, Henry Cabot Lodge Jr. in Pittsburgh, and the president accepting the tributes in Los Angeles.

And the piece of paper in my typewriter was absolutely blank.

But in my in-box appeared a letter:

```
My dear Mr. President,

I have just turned 21 years of age. I am now old enough
to vote and mature enough to take part in political
elections. My problem is, which party am I best suited to
serve? I thought you would be able to help me by telling
me what the Republican Party stands for.

What are its goals and in what way may I help it to
achieve them?

Shirley Jean Havens
Arvada, Colorado
```

Here's the divine intervention part: I had nothing to do with presidential correspondence. The correspondence section at the White House had never before forwarded a letter addressed to the president to me (nor would it ever do so again).

So the president would tell Shirley Jean why she should be a Republican. The president loved the idea, picked up the phone, and asked Aksel Nielson, a Denver banker who was a good friend, to go to Arvada and give him a report on Shirley Jean. (Maybe she was a communist or a drug dealer.) The report came back that Shirley Jean was polite, pretty, a mother of two, and the wife of a plumber. Equally nice: she had written the same letter to Harry Truman and had received a gruff reply to go read a book. Shirley Jean was then invited to the "Dinner with Ike" in Denver so that she could witness (along with *Time* and *Life*) the president's reply to her letter.

After that, she kept writing the president—but of course that wasn't my department.

Get Me Rewrite!

For the speechwriters, the State of the Union Address, delivered by the president before a joint session of Congress in January, is a massive exercise in finding some grid to link all the recommended commitments of the departments of the federal government in a proposed flight plan for the next year. The speech usually goes through thirteen or more drafts. (A draft gets a new number every time the president makes changes.)

That isn't always the case, however, as I can attest. Unbeknown to everyone including President Eisenhower, his address sent to Congress on January 12, 1961, had a simpler history—in terms of drafts. It began the previous spring, when I was told to write a first draft of the 1960 National Republican Platform. The White House understood that the platform ultimately would be the product of the presidential candidate (Richard Nixon) and the party's platform committee. But the White House staff wanted to start the process in a way that ensured Ike's accomplishments would not be overlooked.

The platform went through buffeting changes culminating in the so-called Treaty of Fifth Avenue, when Nixon met Nelson Rockefeller in New York and dictated paragraphs to those of us on the other end of the call at the Blackstone Hotel in Chicago. Nothing was left of my original draft.

Now fast-forward to the end of the Eisenhower administration. The president wanted to give a televised farewell address, now famous for its "military-industrial complex" reference, which he wrote with the aid of Mac Moos and navy captain Ralph Williams. I was assigned to write the State of the Union to be sent to Congress, not read to the Congress by the president. The speech began: "Once again it is my Constitutional duty to assess the state of the Union. On each such previous occasion during the past eight years I have outlined a forward course designed to achieve our mutual objective—a better America in a world of peace. This time my function is different." He would review the record of those past eight years in the hope that, out of the sum of those experiences, lessons useful to the nation would emerge. The rest of President Eisenhower's 1961 State of the Union Address is the first draft of the 1960 Republican Platform that I wrote the previous spring. It made no sense to waste good material.

Calibrating Conflict

The practice of rubbing two advisers together to create sparks was perfected by Franklin D. Roosevelt. Not that you need to worry about not having enough conflict in your administration. There are built-in conflicts: for example, between the State Department (peace) and Defense

Answers:

A. "No new taxes" comes from the title of a Tim Curry album. Peggy Noonan incorporated the phrase into George H. W. Bush's acceptance speech at the 1988 Republican National Convention. In 1990, however, President Bush compromised with Congress and agreed to a tax increase.

B. "Our long national nightmare is over" was written by Robert T. Hartmann for President Gerald Ford's first address to the nation after President Richard Nixon left office in 1974. "Isn't that a little hard on Dick?" wondered Ford, as quoted by Hartmann in his book *Palace Politics* (1980), who threatened to resign if the line was cut. "Junk all the rest of the speech," he remembers saying, "but not that. That is going to be the headline in every paper, the lead in every story."

C. "The military-industrial complex" was in President Dwight Eisenhower's farewell radio and television address of January 17, 1961. In an early draft, speechwriters Malcolm Moos and Ralph Williams warned of the "military-industrial-scientific complex," but science adviser James Killian, the president of MIT, asked for the deletion.

D. "Ask not what your country can do for you," from President John Kennedy's inaugural address, was the hallmark of speechwriter Ted Sorensen's famous contrapuntal style. William Safire in his new edition of *Safire's Political Dictionary* (2008) writes that the "ask not" line may have been modeled on a phrase in an 1884 Memorial Day address delivered by Oliver Wendell Holmes.

E. The "axis of evil," according to President George W. Bush in his January 29, 2002, State of the Union Address, was Iraq, Iran, and North Korea. Speechwriter Matthew Scully, writing in the *Atlantic* (September 2007), claims that the line from speechwriter David Frum was "axis of hatred," and Scully changed "hatred" to "evil." Michael Gerson and John McConnell were the other speechwriters working on the draft.

Department (war), which is why State often pushes for military options and Defense often resists the use of force. And there are always personality clashes that go beyond policy: Reagan's secretary of state, George Shultz, and secretary of defense, Caspar Weinberger, were not fond of each other. (See the "Why Can't We All Just Get Along" section in this chapter for an example of their testy exchanges.)

The advantage of so-called multiple advocacy as a management technique is the expectation that all points of view will be fully

Pick a Presidential Portrait

George Washington by Rembrandt Peale (1741–1827)
*Hung in the Oval Office during the presidencies of George H. W. Bush,
Bill Clinton, and George W. Bush.*

Rarely has multiple advocacy been as clearly set in motion as when President-elect Nixon appointed two Ivy League professors to the White House staff as his senior advisers on domestic policy. A stranger to Nixon, Daniel Patrick Moynihan of Harvard was a liberal whose only intellectual connection to the president may have been that he had recently written scathing criticism of some parts of Lyndon Johnson's Great Society poverty program. Arthur Burns of Columbia was a conservative, a friend, and a sturdy ally of Nixon's during the Eisenhower years when he was chairman of the Council of Economic Advisers. Burns and Moynihan were strong-willed, articulate, and experienced in high-level government combat, and for the first seven months of the new presidency they involved the entire upper reaches of the administration in a war over the Family Assistance Plan, a welfare proposal that Moynihan was pushing—Burns opposing—to guarantee income for poor families with children.

Nixon was frustrated that their long-drawn-out debate was forcing him to wait until August to announce a domestic agenda, well beyond the Hundred Days that presidents like to set for themselves. John Ehrlichman, the president's counsel, noted that Nixon "soon began dreading his appointments with the antagonists. He was never one to enjoy being pulled and hauled upon by special pleaders, and Burns and Moynihan were experts." In the end, Nixon's proposal to Congress was light years removed from anything he had promised in his campaign.

Had Nixon's transition decisions backed him into this corner? He recalls in his memoirs

explained and challenged. This is a worthy aim. While scholars love it, presidents are not as sure that it always serves their purposes. No White House argument stays behind closed doors for long; staff conflicts usually lead to leaks to reporters, which, in turn, can create the impression of an indecisive president. Moreover, dueling arguments for Policy A or Policy B can produce a split-the-difference compromise that lacks the rigor of either A or B.

As Nixon was about to take office in 1969, his speechwriter Ray Price sent him a memo: "For a third of a century, the fashionable critics have been measuring progress according to the standards established by Roosevelt in his first 100 days. If we're going to change the pattern of government, we've got to change the standards of measurement." Nice that Burns's conservatism was meant to be a "counterweight to Moynihan's liberalism." Perhaps. This was written ten years later, and, as with all memoirs, was part of the process of tidying history. My own view—I was deputy to Moynihan and knew Nixon well from previous work—was that there was nothing Hegelian in Nixon's nature or in his management practices up to that time. He tended to place aides in distinct boxes on a chart. Moreover, domestic matters were low priority to a future president dreaming of a breakthrough with Communist China and ending the war in Vietnam. Choosing Burns and Moynihan was important to Nixon for very different reasons unrelated to how the professors would interact and affect policy.

Burns was penciled in to be the next chairman of the Federal Reserve System. It was a term appointment that would not be available until January 1970. What to do with him in the meantime? The answer was to give him cabinet rank, a grand title, and modest duties. (Initially he was to oversee citizen task forces that had been set up during the transition.)

Moynihan was a player in Nixon's desire to lure a prominent Democrat into his administration. Always a partisan figure, Nixon had won an extremely close election. He had asked Senator Henry Jackson to be secretary of defense and was turned down. Moynihan became a prize of considerable worth and was even promised a cabinet-level council somewhat analogous to the National Security Council.

Nixon solved two personnel problems. But I doubt he ever reflected on the price he paid for his inattention to process.

try. But on every Day One Hundred of every new presidency, every presidential scholar in the country will be called by a reporter for his or her assessment of the president's failures.

In this case, multiple advocacy can be the enemy of the demands for prompt action, as Nixon was to find out in a clash between Daniel Patrick Moynihan and Arthur Burns.

Lessons to Apply to Your Transition

When thinking about how much conflict you wish to deliberately build into your staff structure, remember this:

☞ *You can discourage conflict by giving more narrowly drawn titles and duties.*

☞ *Overlapping jurisdictions encourage conflict (see the case in point).*

Why Can't We All Just Get Along?

Every presidency must make its way around many fault lines—some divisions are constitutionally built into the system, some are institutionally arranged within the executive branch, some are promoted by competing outside interests or inspired by the political opposition, and some simply result from the many voices of an open society. That is why the problems presidents make for themselves within their own administrations are so vexing.

Among the most unnecessary arise from personality conflicts. Presidents-in-transition often make appointments having little in the way of personal relationships with their appointees. They have even less knowledge of how unknown official X will interact with unknown official Y—even though X has been slated to become the secretary of state and Y the national security assistant. The appointees' experiences are later recounted in troubling memoirs that often start with a stranger's call to service, as in the opening paragraph of Alexander Haig's *Caveat: Realism, Reagan and Foreign Policy* (Macmillan, 1984): "When, on December 11, 1980, President-elect Ronald Reagan asked me to be his Secretary of State, I had spent no more than three hours alone with him. About an hour of that time had been passed in a Marine helicopter. . . . There was little conversation in the helicopter." A similar passage opens the memoirs of Donald Regan, Reagan's first treasury secretary.

Whatever irritants exist initially within the inner circle are sure to rub raw after staff and media get hold of them, as the following examples illustrate.

Nixon Presidency

> Richard Nixon: "[Secretary of State] Rogers and [Secretary of Defense] Laird occasionally carried on sensitive dealings and negotiations without coordinating them with the White House. . . . [S]ometimes it was done to preclude [National Security Assistant] Kissinger's or my own disapproval; and sometimes, I think, it was done just to show themselves, their departments, and the press that they were capable of independent action. . . .

"Eventually the relationship between Kissinger and Rogers took on a fairly combative aspect. . . . Rogers felt that Kissinger was Machiavellian, deceitful, egotistical, arrogant, and insulting. Kissinger felt that Rogers was vain, uninformed, unable to keep a secret, and hopelessly dominated by the State Department bureaucracy." (Richard Nixon, *RN: The Memoirs of Richard Nixon*, Grosset & Dunlap, 1978)

Henry Kissinger: "Rogers must have considered me an egotistical nitpicker who ruined his relations with [the] President. I tended to view him as an insensitive neophyte who threatened the careful design of our foreign policy. The relationship was bound to deteriorate. Had both of us been wiser we would have understood that we would serve the country best by composing our personal differences and reinforcing each other. . . . But all our attempts to meet regularly foundered. Rogers was too proud. I intellectually too arrogant, and we were both too insecure to adopt a course which would have saved us much needed anguish and bureaucratic headaches." (Henry Kissinger, *The White House Years*, Little, Brown, 1979)

Rogers remained secretary of state into Nixon's second term until September 1973, when he was replaced by Henry Kissinger (who continued to serve also as national security adviser). Nixon then awarded Rogers the Presidential Medal of Freedom.

Carter Presidency

Zbigniew Brzezinski: "[Secretary of State Cyrus Vance's] reluctance to speak up publicly, to provide a broad conceptual explanation for what our Administration was trying to do, and Carter's lack of preparation for doing it himself, pushed me to the forefront. (I will not claim I resisted strongly.) That in turn fueled resentments, if not initially on Cy's part, then clearly so on the part of his subordinates. . . . I was struck, even in the very early months . . . by how much pressure there is from one's own subordinates to engage in conflict with one's principal peers.

"The press seized on these disagreements with a passion and a vengeance. . . . It got to a point that I was not sure whether I was more outraged by pieces portraying Vance as the winner or mortified by ones that celebrated my alleged predominance. . . . [T]he press kept it up, thereby harming everyone concerned, while in fact considerably exaggerating the split between us." (Zbigniew Brzezinski, *Power and*

Principle: Memoirs of the National Security Adviser, 1977–1981, Farrar, Straus and Giroux, 1983)

Vance resigned in April 1980, in protest over the secret mission to rescue American hostages in Iran.

Reagan Presidency

On George Shultz and Caspar Weinberger: "[Secretary of State] Shultz and [Secretary of Defense] Weinberger never had a honeymoon. They were natural rivals, burdened by ancient animosities and a competing view of U.S.-Soviet relations. . . .

"Those who observed the conflict at close hand differed in their assignment of fault but are nearly unanimous in believing that the struggles between these two powerful cabinet secretaries undermined policy coherence and wore down Reagan.

"Neither Shultz nor Weinberger made life easy for Reagan. Weinberger was convinced he knew what Reagan would do if left to his own instincts, and Shultz behaved as if he knew what was best for the president. But the self-indulgent scenes they staged in the president's presence did not bring out the best in Reagan. . . . One can hardly blame him, given this disconcerting example of pettiness that has survived in notes made by an administration official [Arms Control and Disarmament Agency Director Ken Adelman]:

> SHULTZ: I wanted to give you a military opinion on this matter, Mr. President, but I couldn't get one. The secretary of defense wouldn't let me talk to the Joint Chiefs of Staff.
>
> WEINBERGER: You could come to me for the military opinion. My phone number's in the book.
>
> SHULTZ: I wanted another opinion.
>
> WEINBERGER: You could have called me and asked. As I said, my phone number's listed." (Lou Cannon, *President Reagan: The Role of a Lifetime,* Simon & Schuster, 1991)

Weinberger resigned on November 23, 1987; he was indicted for lying in the Iran-Contra case, and subsequently pardoned by President Bush in 1992. Shultz remained Secretary of State until Reagan left office in 1989.

Lesson to Apply to Your Transition

☞ *When making people decisions, ensure interviews and vetting go beyond paper qualifications to questions of personality that could reflect on group dynamics.*

Looking Ahead

Now your White House Office is organized! The boxes are where you want them on the organizational chart and your own people are in the boxes. You can move on: there are simply more interesting matters to engage your attention. Management questions are a bore. At least that was the opinion of most of your predecessors who thought that creating their organization was akin to pinning a butterfly to a corkboard; it will always be there in a pristine state, unless there is a crisis.

Unfortunately, management arrangements are fluid, even under ordinary circumstances. A year from now your organization will be out of shape, more or less. Your staff needs will shift as you move from formulating policies to lobbying your proposals through Congress, then to implementing the new programs. Does your staff adequately reflect the changing circumstances?

People change. They get tired. They develop strong or weak relationships with other people. They leave and are replaced by people with different talents, forming new alliances and rivalries. And, frankly, you cause problems for yourself! Presidents, out of impatience or frustration, often reach out to the person at their elbow to deal with whatever matter is at hand. It's called the Law of Propinquity—and it plays havoc with trying to have a smooth-running organization.

Mark your calendar to reexamine your White House organization one year from today (at the latest).

Perks

Incoming staff should be aware that some perks go along with their jobs. Here are two that are worth looking into:

Great Art

Make a call to the National Gallery as you move into your West Wing office. Request a curator to drop by with suggestions for what paintings you should borrow for your walls.

In 1969, as deputy assistant to the president for urban affairs, I picked a fine Jacob Lawrence, possibly the most famous African American painter of the twentieth century. But my happiest choice was a very large oil by Alma Thomas, a Washington artist, whose bold, irregular yellow dashes filled my days with absolute sunshine. (I sent letters of thanks to all the artists I hung, hoping they would like to know that they had been displayed with satisfaction at the White House.) Next door, New Yorker Pat Moynihan chose a portrait of the cartoonist who brought down the Tweed Ring, Thomas Nast, looking stern and unforgiving. Perhaps Pat's message was that misdeeds would not be permitted here.

Cheap Vacations

There are great places to stay in national parks, including the Virgin Islands. These houses were included in land acquired by the Department of the Interior and are now available to federal officials (in order of rank—White House staff will be bumped by a cabinet member). One site that my family enjoyed—but is no longer available—is Camp Hoover, a group of cabins that Herbert Hoover built on the Rapidan River in Virginia. John Whitaker, who was secretary to the cabinet in the Nixon White House, told me this story about a time he had been fishing there. When a park ranger stopped to chat, Whitaker said, "I understood the camp was built here because President Hoover was a great fisherman. But I've been fishing all morning and I haven't even seen a fish." The ranger replied: "Well, you see, sir, when Mr. Hoover was president, the Secret Service stood at the head of the stream and dropped the trout in."

. . . someone you can't fire"*

*Includes president's parents, siblings, spouse, and children; for the appropriateness of applying this rule to in-laws and vice president's family, contact the editorial board of the *New York Times.*

"Leadership—Bush, Cheney and The Horse," by Pat Oliphant, 2007 (Susan Conway Gallery, Santa Fe, N.M.)

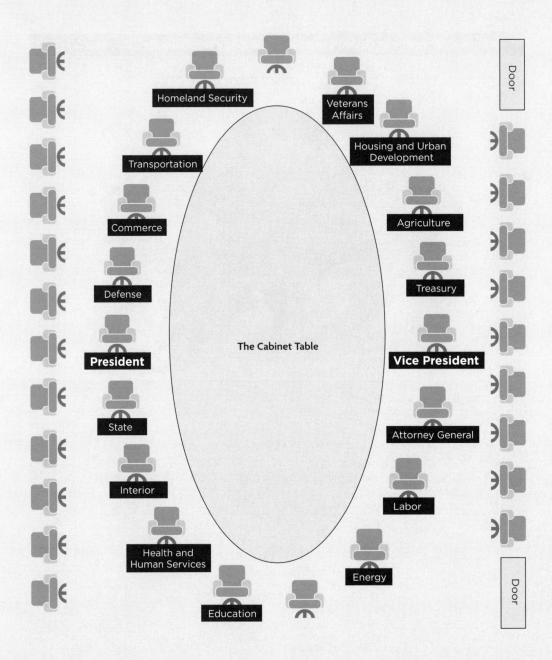

THE CABINET

You have designed and staffed your White House, so you can now effectively move on to choosing your cabinet members and other key officials. You will need to consider the diversity, political, and talent requirements that go into making these choices, including whether you want to reach out to the opposition party. Where are the best pools of talent available to you? What lessons can you learn from the failures of other presidents? And what must be done to get your nominees confirmed by the Senate? These are the questions to which I now turn.

CHAPTER 3

The Cabinet

The "Looks Like America" Cabinet

Cabinet-making for you will be a lot more complicated than it was for Presidents Eisenhower, Kennedy, and Nixon. The original Eisenhower cabinet was dubbed "eight millionaires and a plumber." The millionaires were all white males—as was the plumber, Secretary of Labor Martin Durkin, who had been president of the American Federation of Labor (AFL) Plumbers and Pipe Fitters Union. Eisenhower added a woman to his cabinet, Oveta Culp Hobby, when the Department of Health, Education, and Welfare was created in 1953. She was also white and a millionaire.

The Kennedy and Nixon cabinets were solidly stocked with white men. Kennedy made the "unsubtle gesture" of arranging for Representative William Dawson, an African American, to "decline" his offer of the postmaster-generalship, according to Kennedy adviser Ted Sorensen. (The Post Office was a cabinet department until 1970.) Nixon was turned down by two African Americans: Senator Edward Brooke and Whitney Young, executive director of the Urban League. There is no evidence that he considered appointing a woman or a Hispanic American to a cabinet post. What is remarkable about this period is how little outcry was caused by this absence of diversity.

Carter was the first president-elect to commit himself to a cabinet that "looks like America." Yet by December 15 he still had not appointed an African American or a woman, and he was beginning to feel the heat. "The overwhelming support blacks gave to Mr. Carter—in his primary campaign as well as

> You will have many more opportunities than Presidents Eisenhower and Kennedy to make cabinet appointments. Since 1965 the government has been on a department-creating binge: Housing and Urban Development (1965), Transportation (1966), Energy (1977), Veterans Affairs (1988), and Homeland Security (2003). In 1979 the Department of Housing, Education, and Welfare (HEW) was split into Housing and Human Services (HHS), and Education.

Up against the Walls

Behind the president and across from him, behind the vice president, are rows of chairs. When the cabinet meets, who sits in them? The answer shown below is from a cabinet meeting of President George H. W. Bush (note seating differences in the Bush II cabinet, page 58).

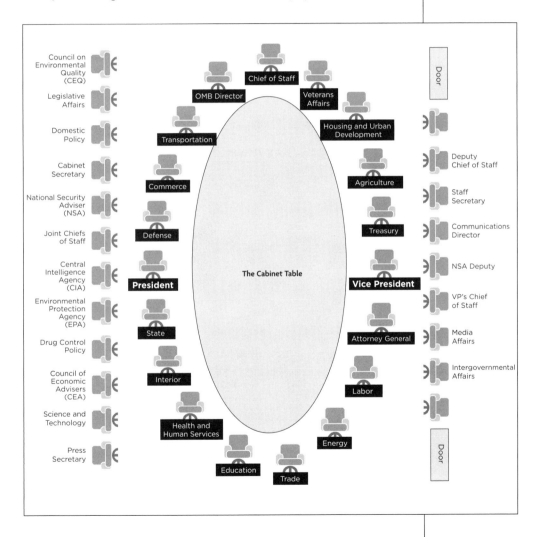

in the general election—marks the first time a president has been so in-debted to a minority community," wrote a *New York Times* reporter, "and blacks fully expect appropriate payoffs."

Carter's first appointment of an African American was Representa-tive Andrew Young of Atlanta to be U.S. ambassador to the United Nations. The problem for Carter was that having filled his "inner cabi-net" (State, Treasury, Defense, and Justice) with white men, advocates for women and minorities complained that their constituents were be-ing treated with disrespect by being offered only "outer cabinet" posi-tions. This issue would have greater consequences for the next Demo-cratic president.

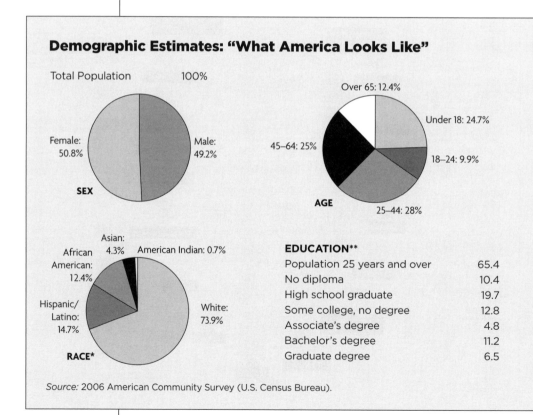

Demographic Estimates: "What America Looks Like"

Total Population **100%**

SEX
- Female: 50.8%
- Male: 49.2%

AGE
- Over 65: 12.4%
- Under 18: 24.7%
- 18–24: 9.9%
- 25–44: 28%
- 45–64: 25%

RACE*
- African American: 12.4%
- Asian: 4.3%
- American Indian: 0.7%
- Hispanic/Latino: 14.7%
- White: 73.9%

EDUCATION**

Population 25 years and over	65.4
No diploma	10.4
High school graduate	19.7
Some college, no degree	12.8
Associate's degree	4.8
Bachelor's degree	11.2
Graduate degree	6.5

Source: 2006 American Community Survey (U.S. Census Bureau).

No president-elect worked as hard as Bill Clinton to fit all the pieces—geography, ideology, politics, gender, ethnicity—into the cabinet puzzle. When he announced at a press conference on November 12, 1992, that "my cabinet will look more like America than previous administrations," it was as if he were making representation the theme of his transition. On December 9 the *New York Times* wrote that Clinton was seeking a woman for attorney general. As the process dragged on, according to insider George Stephanopoulos, "the transition team was scrambling to find the best female attorney general rather than the best attorney general period."

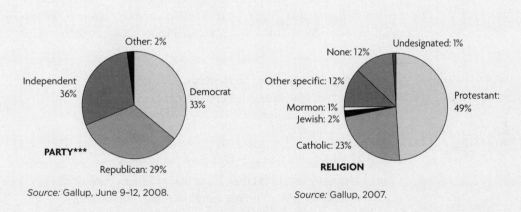

Source: Gallup, June 9–12, 2008.

Source: Gallup, 2007.

 * These numbers add up to more than 100% because of multiracial Americans who checked off more than one box on the form.

 ** The "education" question was only asked of the 65.4% of Americans age 25 and over, but the percentages here represent percent of total Americans.

 *** This does not reflect actual party registration numbers, but a response to the question "Do you consider yourself a Republican, a Democrat, or an independent?"

Clinton's first choice, Zoë Baird, had to withdraw when it was revealed that she and her husband, a Yale Law School professor, had hired illegal immigrants as household help and had not paid the Social Security tax on their employment. Clinton's second choice, U.S. district court judge Kimba Wood, also had employed an undocumented immigrant as a nanny. Clinton's third choice, Janet Reno, was finally confirmed by the Senate on March 11. The situation reminded journalist R. W. Apple Jr. of Casey Stengel's famous lament to the 1962 Mets: "Can't anybody here play this game?"

Inner cabinet diversity, on the other hand, was never much of an issue for President-elect George W. Bush, since it was clear from the early stages that Colin Powell, the former chairman of the Joint Chiefs of Staff and an African American, would be his pick for secretary of state.

Yet it is obvious that you are going to spend a lot of your transition seeking balances that create a "Looks Like America" cabinet. When weighing diversity as a cabinet standard, consider these pros and cons:

Pros
- Broad representation on your policymaking team.
- Payback to the constituencies that elected you.
- Symbolism of inclusiveness.

Cons
- Risk of creating the appearance that a nominee's gender, race, or religion is more important than his or her qualifications to do the job.
- Risk of angering groups whose candidates are not selected.
- Risk of painting yourself into a corner.

How to Expand Your Cabinet

Beyond the mandatory department secretaries, you can put anyone you want in your cabinet. With the stroke of a pen, President Carter added his UN ambassador, Andrew Young, to his cabinet. The UN post had been given cabinet rank twice before. Eisenhower bestowed it on Henry Cabot Lodge Jr., one of the president's early supporters who had just lost his

Senate seat to John F. Kennedy. As president-elect in 1960, Kennedy gave it to Adlai Stevenson, his party's presidential candidate in 1952 and 1956, who would rather have been Kennedy's secretary of state.

President Clinton added three women to his cabinet: Madeleine Albright (UN ambassador), Laura D'Andrea Tyson (Council of Economic Advisers), and Carol Browner (EPA administrator). Clinton also made cabinet members out of the drug czar, the director of the Small Business Administration, and the director of the Federal Emergency Management Agency. As a result, it was hard to fit them all around the cabinet table.

If recent history is any indication, you are most likely to give cabinet status to your chief of staff, OMB director, and trade representative. Note that President George H. W. Bush, who had been both UN representative and CIA director, chose not to put either in his cabinet. The CIA, he felt, "should not be in the policy business," and "there is no point in the United Nations Ambassador sitting around, as I did for a while, talking about ag policy."

The Add-on Cabinet Officials

Appointee	Post
Eisenhower (1953)	
Henry Cabot Lodge Jr.	Ambassador to the United Nations
Kennedy (1961)	
Adlai Stevenson	Ambassador to the United Nations
Nixon (1969)	
Arthur Burns	Counselor to the president
Carter (1977)	
Zbigniew Brzezinski	Adviser to the president on National Security Affairs
Bert Lance	Director, Office of Management and Budget
Charles L. Schultze	Chairman, Council of Economic Advisers
Andrew Young	Ambassador to the United Nations
Reagan (1981)	
William E. Brock III	U.S. Trade Representative
William J. Casey	Director, Central Intelligence Agency
Jeane J. Kirkpatrick	Ambassador to the United Nations
Edwin A. Meese III	Counselor to the president

continued

Appointee	Post
George H. W. Bush (1989)	
Richard G. Darman	Director, Office of Management and Budget
Carla A. Hills	U.S. Trade Representative
Clinton (1993)	
Madeleine K. Albright	Ambassador to the United Nations
Lee P. Brown	Director, Office of National Drug Control Policy
Carol M. Browner	Administrator, Environmental Protection Agency
Michael Kantor	U.S. Trade Representative
Thomas F. "Mack" McLarty	Chief of staff
Leon E. Panetta	Director, Office of Management and Budget
Laura D'Andrea Tyson	Chair, Council of Economic Advisers
George W. Bush (2001)	
Andrew Card Jr.	Chief of staff
Mitchell E. Daniels Jr.	Director, Office of Management and Budget
Christine Todd Whitman	Administrator, Environmental Protection Agency
Robert B. Zoellick	U.S. Trade Representative

Check out presidential transitions on the Brookings website (www.brookings.edu/transition) for profiles of the start-up cabinets of Presidents Eisenhower (1953), Kennedy (1961), Nixon (1969), Carter (1977), Reagan (1981), George H. W. Bush (1989), Clinton (1993), and George W. Bush (2001). Who picked governors? From which states? And senators? What schools were the academics from? Who was the oldest cabinet member? The youngest? Who was the attorney general who later became secretary of state? Which presidents put the party chairman in the cabinet? Lots of data!

The Original Cabinets: Eisenhower to George W. Bush

Follow the fascinating progression of presidents' start-up cabinets over the past half-century, using the chart on page 67. From the all-white cabinets of Presidents Eisenhower, Kennedy, and Nixon to the two most recent presidents, Democrat Bill Clinton and Republican George W. Bush, who chose men and women—mostly men—only half of whom were of white European origin.

The Start-up Cabinets: Race (other than European-origin white)

Eisenhower (1953)	None
Kennedy (1961)	None
Nixon (1969)	None
Carter (1977)	Patricia R. Harris, African American (HUD)
Reagan (1981)	Samuel Pierce, African American (HUD)
George H. W. Bush (1989)	Manuel Lujan, Hispanic (Interior) Louis Sullivan, African American (HUD) Lauro D. Cavazos, Hispanic (Education)
Clinton (1993)	Mike Espy, African American (Agriculture) Ronald H. Brown, African American (Commerce) Hazel O'Leary, African American (Energy) Henry G. Cisneros, Hispanic (HUD) Federico F. Peña, Hispanic (Transportation) Donna E. Shalala, Lebanese American (HHS) Jesse Brown, African American (Veterans)
George W. Bush (2001)	Colin Powell, African American (State) Elaine Chao, Asian American (Commerce) Spencer Abraham, Lebanese American (Energy) Mel Martinez, Hispanic (HUD) Rod Paige, African American (Education) Norman Mineta, Asian American (Transportation)

Talent Hunt

Now comes the moment when you must find the people to head the fifteen departments and the major agencies of the federal government.

Look at what you are asking executives to manage: the smallest department (in terms of budget) is Commerce, which will be authorized to spend nearly $9 billion a year during your presidency; the largest, Health and Human Services, will have budget authority of more than $765 billion. You have only a four-year contract, once renewable, so you will want leaders who can get things done in a hurry. Yet the Congress—from which your departments receive their money—also has ideas about how the departments should be run, as has the civil service, which can wait out the appointed officials. Meanwhile, the media are poised to enjoy any false step.

The Start-up Cabinets: Eisenhower to George W. Bush

Gender

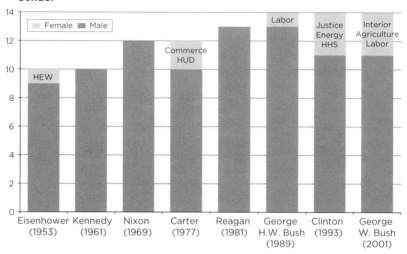

Average Age

Note how most presidents-elect seem to have a "comfort zone" in which they pick cabinet officials from their own age cohort.

Almost everyone you ask to serve is making a lot more money than the $191,300 salary a cabinet officer gets. Yet you will usually get the people you want for the "inner cabinet"—State, Treasury, Defense, and Justice. Beyond that, it can be difficult: President Reagan was turned down by six of his first choices—five for "outer cabinet" jobs. President Nixon endured four rejections (Kissinger says there was a fifth). If your choices turn you down, don't twist arms: those who say no usually have a good reason for not taking the job, even if it may not sound like a good reason to you.

As you proceed with your talent hunt, powerful groups will take a keen interest in which way you appear to be leaning. When it became known that President-elect Carter was weighing the merits of Harold Brown or James Schlesinger for secretary of defense, there was a sudden campaign for Paul Warnke. Its purpose was to position Brown, who had been deputy secretary of defense in the Johnson administration, as a moderate compromise between the liberal Warnke and conservative Schlesinger, who had held the secretary of defense position under Presidents Nixon and Ford. Washington games such as this can provide you with hints of candidates' strengths and weaknesses.

Here are five suggestions on where to look for the kinds of officials who have been productive in the past.

University and College Presidents

The job of university president closely resembles that of running a government department. As with cabinet officers, these administrators have more *responsibility* than *authority*. (You might find a way of asking them and other candidates for your cabinet, "What have you accomplished without formal authority?") They have learned how to deal with ambiguity, which corporate executives often find disquieting. They have also learned to deal with competing constituencies (trustees, faculty, students, administrators, alumni, the local community, and, in the case of public institutions, legislative bodies).

Review the records of the following university presidents who went on to have successful stints in government: Edward Levi, University of Chicago, attorney general (Ford); Harold Brown, Cal Tech, secretary of defense (Carter), Donna Shalala, University of Wisconsin–Madison, secretary of health and human services (Clinton).

Governors

All incoming presidents since Eisenhower have picked at least one governor (Kennedy and Nixon each picked three), but hardly ever for the inner cabinet. Western governors have been popular choices for interior secretary.

The record of governors as cabinet secretaries is a mixed bag: Orville Freeman of Minnesota, secretary of agriculture for Presidents Kennedy and Johnson, and Richard Riley of South Carolina, Clinton's secretary of education, were outstanding. Another South Carolina governor, James Edwards, barely lasted a year as Reagan's secretary of energy; and Nixon had to fire Alaskan Walter Hickel, another western governor at interior.

Members of Congress

Watch out for members of Congress: management is rarely their forte. Although some may have had business experience before arriving in Washington, law is more likely their occupation. Their skill is in lobbying former colleagues (defense secretaries Mel Laird and Dick Cheney were notably effective in this manner). If you go with legislators, be sure to pair them with talented managers as their deputies. You will be much better off if you select the deputies yourself—as long as the cabinet officials feel they can live with your choices. This creates a sort of "double veto" system.

Business

The size of government agencies might suggest that the natural choices for these executive positions reside in corporate America. The answer is yes and no, depending on factors such as whether the executives have spent their entire careers in one company (not good prospects), whether their type of company has extensive contact with or regulation by the government (useful prospects), and whether their résumés also show substantial community involvement, such as being a school board chair (very good prospects).

Faux Bipartisanship

In the "tradition" of bipartisanship, you will be urged to appoint people from the opposition party either to your cabinet or other prominent positions—especially if you just won a close election. Some of these officials will give you good service, but not because they voted for your opponent.

How far Nixon went during the 1968 transition to get a Democrat into his administration is illustrated by his negotiations with Sargent Shriver, President Kennedy's brother-in-law. After being offered the UN post, according to Nixon's memoirs, Shriver "required a pledge that the federal poverty programs would not be cut." Such meddling in domestic affairs was too much for the president-elect, who told William Rogers, his secretary of state–designate, "to inform Shriver that I have decided against him and to let him know why." Shriver then tried, unsuccessfully, to backpedal.

President-elect Kennedy had more success in luring Douglas Dillon, a Republican with a distinguished record in public service, to be his secretary of the treasury, thus easing the fears of Wall Street. He also made Henry Cabot Lodge Jr., Nixon's running mate in the 1960 presidential election, U.S. ambassador to Vietnam, a convenient place to put a Republican if things got too hot.

Such actions do not violate the Trading with the Enemy Act, but neither do they buy what is usually their intended purpose—bipartisan support. The Republican in a Democratic administration, or vice versa, is typically viewed as a turncoat. As Clinton's secretary of state Madeleine Albright accurately observes in her book *Memo to the President Elect* (HarperCollins, 2008), "Such an appointment will provide more the appearance of bipartisanship than the reality."

Two questions to ask yourself before appointing a Democrat (Republican) to your Republican (Democratic) administration:

1. **What do I expect to gain by appointing this person?**

    _____

    _____

2. **Is this the best person for the job—regardless of party?**

    ❏ Yes, definitely.   ❏ No, we can do better.

Being too rich can also pose a "problem." How to divest assets in order to conform to standards of public service? Charles E. Wilson of General Motors and Ford's Robert McNamara sold their stock in the companies they ran before becoming secretaries of defense. But this was more difficult for Hewlett-Packard cofounder David Packard, who owned 29 percent of the company's stock when Nixon chose him to be deputy secretary of defense in 1969. Packard could not dump his stock on the market without penalizing the other shareholders. He finally proposed putting his stock in a trust with all income and increase in value going to educational and charitable institutions. The Senate then confirmed him.

Government

The safest place to look for good cabinet officials is among those who have already been good cabinet officials—the repeaters. There are people in both parties, as well as others who have served under presidents of both parties, who have already proved their worth. Take a look at a résumé like that of the late Elliot Richardson, the only person who ever held four cabinet-level positions: secretary of health, education, and welfare; secretary of defense; attorney general; and secretary of commerce. And for good measure, he had also been under secretary of state. Richardson was not an expert in welfare policy or commerce; his expertise was in running large government departments. You cannot go wrong with people like Richardson.

One of the strangest discoveries about selecting cabinet officials has to do with how well presidents know their appointees. You might assume that the better you know your pick, the more likely you will pick the right person for the job. But it does not necessarily work that way. Nixon's closest friend in his cabinet was Robert Finch, the secretary of health, education, and welfare. At the other extreme, Nixon's notes to himself at the time he was making his cabinet announcements show that he didn't know the first name or how to spell the last name of George Shultz, his pick for labor secretary. Finch was a disaster and had to be removed to the White House staff, where he wasn't given much to do; Shultz was so successful that Nixon later elevated him to the inner cabinet.

Once you have settled on a choice for a cabinet post and your vetters have done their work, dispassionately assess your nominee's chances at confirmation by the Senate:

- If the vetting process raised no red flags, proceed to "When to Grovel."

- If there might be trouble with this nomination, skip forward to "When to Fold."

Idea to Apply to Your Transition

☞ *Start your selection process by asking those who have held cabinet positions to tell you the qualities necessary for success and what you should avoid.*

When to Grovel

Although confirmation hearings are conducted by different Senate committees filled with different interests and egos, you have probably noticed something holistic about the way senators deal with a new president's initial slate of appointments.

Perhaps the energy expended in fighting one nominee cannot be recycled.

Perhaps there is a point past which opposition is perceived as obstructionism and becomes politically counterproductive.

The result is that you will get a lot of brushfires, but only one truly horrendous conflagration. Senators seem to demand that there always be one. Perhaps you should designate one of your appointees to be the sacrificial lamb so that the others can survive unscathed. (Just joking!)This is the way it worked for two of George W. Bush's nominees. His choice for attorney general, Senator John Ashcroft, had well-documented, deeply controversial views on abortion, gun control, and the death penalty. The nomination produced weeks of anguished debate before he was finally confirmed, 58 to 42, on February 1. The brouhaha probably eased the confirmation of Bush's candidate for interior secretary, Gail Norton, who should have been equally controversial. Environmentalists waged a fierce fight, but it had little effect on the Senate and Norton was comfortably approved, 75 to 24.

The experiences of cabinet appointees Ashcroft and Norton—being challenged on the basis of their policy beliefs rather than personal behavior—is a relatively new phenomenon, going back no further perhaps than Nixon's appointment of interior secretary Walter Hickel, a business-oriented governor of Alaska who was accused of being insensitive to conservation. The rule of thumb for that earlier time was that, given minimum ethical standards, a president was entitled to his

"We're dead meat"
Cartoon by Ann Telnaes, used with permission

choice, since the appointee served only at his pleasure and would not be passed on to the next president. Those were the good old days.

In response to more and more confirmation fights, a group has emerged in Washington known as the sherpas, who have turned steering nominees through the confirmation progress into a fine art. There are Republican sherpas and Democratic sherpas. It's not exactly a club, but they are known to each other. Sign up the ones you need early.

Your nominees should be prepared to explain themselves. One of the more painful experiences befell Dr. Louis Sullivan, George H. W. Bush's choice for secretary of health and human services, who was twice forced to reverse course to get in line with his president's position. Belatedly, the White House staff put him through a cram course (known in Washington parlance as a "murder board") to simulate how he would be grilled by the senators.

Your nominees will need to understand what most worries the senators on their oversight and appropriating committees. Before Brock Adams, Carter's choice for transportation secretary, could be confirmed, Senator Daniel Patrick Moynihan of New York made sure he promised to meet with northeastern governors to discuss the possibilities of using a large portion of their highway money for mass transportation and would review federal support for the Westway highway project in lower Manhattan.

Your nominees will have to endure being confronted by growl and swagger. (Every Senate committee seems to have a designated growler.) This is no easy task for nominees who also have a similarly high sense of self-importance. The best advice for the poor souls who come from pursuits other than the political is to smile and grovel. In the end, the senators will give you pretty much what you ask for—but only once your nominees have given them the respect they think they deserve.

Idea to Apply to Your Transition

☞ *Advise your nominees that their long-term success may require suffering short-term pain.*

Pick a Presidential Portrait

Andrew Jackson after Thomas Sully (1783–1872)
*Hung in the Oval Office during the presidencies of Richard Nixon,
Ronald Reagan, George H. W. Bush, and Bill Clinton.*

When to Fold

Life would be much easier for presidents-in-transition if only their personnel selection process could test for the five criteria laid out by Pendleton James, a corporate headhunter who was in charge of recruitment for President-elect Reagan:

1. Commitment to the president's philosophy and program.

2. The highest integrity and personal qualifications.

3. Experience and skills that fit the task.

4. No personal agenda that conflicts with being a member of the president's team.

5. The toughness needed to withstand the pressures and inducements of Washington and to accomplish the changes sought by the president.

So you follow this prescription, you think you have the person you want, and suddenly there's a problem. Why? Most likely one of two things has happened.

Inadequate Vetting

Inadequate vetting—the failure to dig deep enough to get the troubling information—was what caused problems for President Carter (in the case of Kennedy administration veteran Ted Sorensen), Clinton (in the case of Lani Guinier), and George W. Bush (in the case of Linda Chavez).

Nominated to be CIA director, Sorensen's offense was that he took classified material with him when he left the White House after Kennedy's assassination to write a book.

Guinier, nominated to be assistant attorney general in charge of the civil rights division, had expressed views in her writings that were, Clinton wrote in his memoirs, "in conflict with my support for affirmative action and opposition to quotas." He withdrew the nomination, saying he had not been aware of her views.

Chavez, nominated to be secretary of labor, had taken a battered woman into her home, an illegal immigrant from Guatemala, who did occasional chores and had been given at least $1,500. Chavez had not provided this information to Bush's vetters or the FBI. After her name was withdrawn, Bush announced a replacement nominee just two days later. In Washington he was given more credit for acting expeditiously than blame for making a flawed appointment. It probably also helped that the new nominee (Elaine Chao) was married to a prominent Republican senator.

Insufficient Understanding of Political Risks

Not realizing or understanding the political risks of a particular nominee is what caused problems for Nixon (in the case of Dr. John Knowles, who was to be nominated as assistant secretary for health until the American Medical Association, which disliked Knowles's support for universal health care, opposed him), George H. W. Bush (in the case of John Tower; see page 80), and Clinton (in the case of Zoë Baird).

Remember Zoë Baird, the candidate for attorney general who had employed illegal aliens as household help? Surely this belongs in the category of inadequate vetting. Not so, according to Clinton: "The employment of illegal immigrants was not that uncommon then," he wrote in his memoirs, and Baird had not tried to conceal the information. "We had simply underestimated its significance." This miscalculation caused her to endure a brutal confirmation hearing:

Senator Thurmond: You admit you did wrong?

Baird: Yes.

Thurmond: You're sorry you did wrong?

Baird: Absolutely.

Thurmond: You're repentant for doing wrong?

Baird: Yes, sir.

Baird's nomination was withdrawn.

The Baird case also should remind us how repeatedly presidents-elect have been in trouble because they acted contrary to information that was known to them. Mack McLarty "told me he would prefer another job more suited to his business background," Clinton wrote. "Nevertheless, I pressed Mack to accept the [chief of staff] position." Paul O'Neill met with George W. Bush and Dick Cheney and outlined all the reasons he should not be appointed treasury secretary. He cited policy positions that he favored and they opposed, such as a heavy tax on gasoline. Most important, he said that after years of running Alcoa, "I think it might be hard to take a staff job."

"Bush laughed. Dick laughed," according to the account O'Neill gave to Ron Suskind in *The Price of Loyalty* (Simon & Schuster, 2004). "We know all that stuff," Bush said. "Doesn't matter. We want you to take the job."

O'Neill's reasons for not taking the job accurately reflected what was to happen and why he was fired. Most of these cases begin as loose threads that, when pulled, unravel the whole garment. The classified material in the Sorensen case was the thread, in itself not necessarily disqualifying. But others soon were pulling: Republicans and elements of the Democratic Party not friendly to the Kennedys, intelligence community professionals who objected to his lack of experience in the field and his status as a conscientious objector in World War II, and information that his law firm represented certain foreign governments. At his confirmation hearing, Sorensen did exactly what he knew had to be done. He folded. He escaped with his reputation intact. Carter had his mandatory Senate defeat, caused by his staff's insufficient vetting.

The most significant failed nomination is that of John Tower, the former senator from Texas, whom George H. W. Bush nominated to be secretary of defense. He would not fold. His nomination was not defeated until March, causing three other cabinet confirmations to be delayed.

Idea to Apply to Your Transition

☞ *When a nomination is in trouble, count votes and move quickly.*

Case in Point: The Tower Nomination

John Tower was no innocent traveler in the Washington wilderness. He had retired from the Senate in 1985 after 24 years of service. As the virtual founder of the modern Republican Party in Texas, Tower had long supported George H. W. Bush's political aspirations and had stuck with him through some difficult times. His knowledge of the Pentagon was profound. He badly wanted to be secretary of defense. Confirmation would be easy: the Senate has the reputation of a clubby place, and rejection of a cabinet nomination had happened only eight times in 200 years.

On February 23, 1989, the Armed Service Committee, the committee Tower had once chaired, split along party lines and voted down his nomination, 11 to 9. During the committee hearings Tower was subjected to an almost daily barrage of allegations about drinking and womanizing, with other charges leveled against his defense industry connections. On March 9 the full Senate rejected Tower, 53 to 47, with three Democrats voting for him and one Republican voting against. It was the first time in history that an incoming president had been denied a cabinet member of his choice.

The administration had put too much faith in the Senate's habit of looking out for its own. (Only one former senator had ever been denied a cabinet seat, and that was in 1868.) Its own handling of the nomination was remarkably incompetent, given how many of the Bush people were experienced Washington hands who had served under President Reagan. Moreover, at a key moment, the president and his top aides were away in Japan for Emperor Hirohito's funeral. When Committee Chairman Sam Nunn finally concluded that Tower's drinking problem made him unfit to stand in the chain of command of the nuclear arsenal, nothing could be done to get the nominee through the Democratic Senate.

Bush had stood by his man—as Carter had *not* with Sorensen, and as Clinton had *not* with Guinier. Some honored him for going down fighting, even if incompetently. But he paid a heavy price for the Tower humiliation.

Failures

Cabinet selection is guesswork; it's about future performance. You try hard to improve your odds. You ask people you respect and trust to propose names or comment on candidates, you interview finalists and ask the right questions, you turn to experienced vetters to review the files. And a year later you know you appointed the wrong person. In some cases, your mistake is serious.

Here are three appointments to the highest posts in government—State, Defense, and Treasury. All three had brilliant careers yet were fired by the presidents who appointed them. The failures, in this context, were the presidents.

To demonstrate, I construct mock "personal selection forms" for the three in question: Alexander Haig, appointed secretary of state by President-elect Ronald Reagan (1980); Les Aspin, appointed secretary of defense by President-elect Bill Clinton (1992); and Paul O'Neill, appointed secretary of the treasury by President-elect George W. Bush (2000). These are followed by mock "performance evaluations" presenting evidence that led the presidents to reverse course (it consists only of information that was or could have been known to the appointers at the time).

The exercise concludes with an assessment (also based on the evidence at hand or evidence that could have been assembled at the time) of whether the presidents should have made the appointments. Two of them seemed ill suited from the outset; the third failure remains a mystery (at least to me).

Personnel Selection Form
Reagan Transition, December 1980

OFFICE: Secretary of State

CANDIDATE: Alexander M. Haig Jr.

CAREER SUMMARY: Born in Philadelphia, Pennsylvania, 1924

B.S., United States Military Academy, 1947
M.A. (international relations), Georgetown University, 1961
Service in Korea, awarded two Silver Stars
Service in Vietnam, awarded Distinguished Service Cross
Deputy assistant to president for national security affairs, 1970–73
White House chief of staff, 1973–74
NATO commander, 1974–79
Retired from U.S. Army as four-star general, 1979
CEO, United Technologies, 1979 to present

ASSESSMENT:

Management
Noted as excellent manager since his days as a young officer on
General Douglas MacArthur's staff in Japan.

Expertise
Obviously knows Department of Defense matters, but also well versed
in all national security aspects from his days as Henry Kissinger's
deputy in the Nixon White House.

Political Skills
As Nixon's chief of staff, Haig credited with keeping government
running during Watergate scandal. Nixon gives highest recommendation
to be secretary of state.

Loyalty
Your advisers fear he wants to run for president. Haig claims this
is not true at this time.

Personal
Known to have a temper. Otherwise, high marks.

DECISION: Hired

Performance Evaluation for President Reagan

July 1982
Alexander Haig
Secretary of State

Secretary Haig has publicly accused the White House staff of waging a "guerrilla campaign" against him. Chief of Staff James Baker, Deputy Chief of State Mike Deaver, and policy adviser Ed Meese all find him difficult to work with. You have personally talked with the secretary and your former national security adviser (NSA), Dick Allen, about their conflicts. Apparently matters are not much better between Haig and your new NSA, Bill Clark. He has asked you to fire UN Ambassador Jeane Kirkpatrick, which you refused to do. His displeasures appear to be more about people than about policy, although he contends otherwise. He believes, for instance, that you are unhappy with his policy of shuttle diplomacy in the Falklands War, which is not true.

He repeatedly claims his status is being undercut and his turf encroached upon. Some concerns relate to matters of protocol. Most recently he complained about his accommodations on *Air Force One* and about not being assigned to your helicopter on the flight from Heathrow to London. You have witnessed repeated displays of his temper. He is once again threatening to resign.

DECISION:
The president will inform Secretary Haig that he has accepted his resignation.

Personnel Selection Form

Clinton Transition, December 1992

OFFICE: Secretary of Defense

CANDIDATE: Leslie "Les" Aspin Jr.

CAREER SUMMARY: Born in Milwaukee, Wisconsin, 1938

B.A., summa cum laude, Yale University, 1960
M.A., Oxford University, 1962 (Rhodes Scholar)
Ph.D., economics, Massachusetts Institute of Technology, 1966
Officer, U.S. Army, 1966—68
Systems analyst in the Pentagon (one of McNamara's "whiz kids")
Member, U.S. House of Representatives, 1971 to present
Chairman, House Armed Services Committee, 1985 to present

ASSESSMENT:

Management
No experience in management other than running a small congressional office. Not necessarily a problem: another Wisconsin representative, Mel Laird, did well as defense secretary under President Nixon.

Expertise
Important consideration, given that the president-elect has no military experience. Senator Sam Nunn will not accept the appointment, leaving Aspin the leading expert available. However, some of his positions worry General Colin Powell and others in the military.

Political Skills
Excellent congressional district relations. Occasional problems with Democratic House colleagues over support for opposition policies (MX missile and aid to Nicaraguan Contras in 1987; support for military force in Kuwait in 1991). Still, expect a smooth confirmation.

Loyalty
Not in Clinton's inner circle ("FOB"). But was a campaign adviser.

Personal
No known John Tower—type problems. Divorced. Rumored to be dating a *New York Times* reporter. Said to be in good health.

DECISION: Hired

Performance Evaluation for President Clinton

December 1993
Les Apsin
Secretary of Defense

Secretary Aspin had difficulty dealing with your gays-in-the-military commitment. His contradictory comments on national TV contributed to the initial confusion about the policy. He also had problems on policy revisions that would allow servicewomen to serve in combat situations. Personnel matters are apparently not his strong suit.

Serious heart ailment, February 1993; pacemaker implantation the next month. His style seems to make the Joint Chiefs uncomfortable: late for meetings, unfiltered dialogue, a preference for analysis over decision. Bob Woodward has written in the *Washington Post* that "the starkest skeptics fear that Clinton has sent Hamlet, the Prince of Reconsideration, to the Pentagon."

Aspin's role in the Haiti fiasco last October demands review. You approved the plan to send the USS *Harlan County,* carrying 200 troops, to Port-au-Prince to help reinstate President Aristide. When met by a jeering mob, our ship turned around and came home. Hardly our finest hour. The point is that Aspin opposed the action yet refused to press his objections. Why? Some think that as an outsider—different as such from your National Security Council adviser and secretary of state—he feels hesitant to push his positions.

Now we have Black Hawk Down. The secretary acknowledges that he erred in not granting General Powell's request to reinforce the U.S. commander in Somalia with tanks, armored vehicles, and AC-130 Spectre gunships. Eighteen U.S. soldiers are dead in Mogadishu, and more than seventy-five wounded.

DECISION:
We will announce the resignation of the secretary of defense on December 15, 1993, for personal reasons.

Personnel Selection Form

George W. Bush Transition, December 2000

OFFICE: Secretary of the Treasury

CANDIDATE: Paul H. O'Neill

CAREER SUMMARY: Born in St. Louis, Missouri, 1935

B.A., economics, Fresno State College, California, 1960
M.P.A., Indiana University, 1966
Computer systems analyst, Veterans Administration, 1961–66
Joined U.S. Office of Management and Budget, 1967
Deputy director of OMB, 1974–77
Vice president, International Paper Company, 1977–85
President, International Paper Company, 1985–87
Chairman and CEO, Alcoa, 1987-99

ASSESSMENT:

Management
Highest rating in both U.S. government and private industry. But has been out of government for nearly twenty-five years.

Expertise
Brilliant record at Alcoa. But background in manufacturing sector concerns Wall Street and financial services industry. Close to Fed Chairman Alan Greenspan.

Political Skills
Blunt style. Vocal and controversial stands—on issues such as global warming and gas tax—that are not in keeping with the views of the president-elect. However, highly recommended by Cheney.

Loyalty
No personal history with president-elect (they met once).
No contribution to campaign.

Personal
Dedicated family man. Deeply involved in community service. Will have to take multimillion-dollar stock-option loss on entering government.

DECISION: Hired

Performance Evaluation for President George W. Bush

December 2002
Paul O'Neill
Secretary of the Treasury

Almost from the beginning, Secretary O'Neill has committed a series of indiscretions, such as telling the *Wall Street Journal* that Wall Street professionals are "people who sit in front of a flickering green screen" and "are not the sort of people you would want to help you think about complex questions." The *Los Angeles Times* has characterized him as "a man who has elevated candor to a martial art." Others have called him "refreshingly candid."

   He has not been available during several stock market meltdowns. On one such occasion, he was in Africa with Irish rock star Bono.

   His relations are strained with several cabinet members who feel he is trying to poach on their territory, notably EPA administrator Christine Whitman and Education Secretary Rod Paige. It is also rumored that House Ways and Means Chairman Bill Thomas is not speaking to him. It is an inescapable conclusion that O'Neill has a tin ear for politics.

   The big problem, of course, is that the secretary did not get behind our 2001 economic stimulus package, and he has made it clear that he could not publicly support the second round of tax cuts that you will be proposing.

DECISION:
Tell Vice President Cheney to call Secretary O'Neill and ask him to resign.

In Retrospect

Should the presidents have made the hiring decisions they made?

President Reagan: Secretary of State Alexander Haig

"I had admired Haig very much and respected his performance as commander of NATO," Reagan wrote in his memoir, *An American Life* (Simon & Schuster, 1990), "and [I] selected him as my secretary of state because of this record and his experience in Washington during the Nixon years." But Reagan's experience with Haig in government left him somewhat less enamored: "The Al Haig who was my secretary of state wasn't the same Al Haig I met when he was at NATO."

Put aside Haig's petulant reactions to what he perceived as slights. They did him no good. But those in powerful positions have been known before to be offensive. Rather, Haig, who as Nixon's chief of staff had been so brilliant at the center of one of the country's greatest political crises, had now been defeated in minor combat. Nothing in the Reagan administration of 1981–82 was remotely comparable to the Machiavellian intrigues of life in the final days of Watergate, when James Rosen, John Mitchell's biographer, considered Haig "perhaps the era's shrewdest practitioner of palace politics." Yet Haig was unable to understand, win over, run over, or get around the wall of assistants that defined how Reagan chose to manage his presidency.

Reagan was right. Al Haig wasn't the person he had a right to expect. So Reagan did the best that a transitioning president could do: he made his choice for the right reason—and it turned out to be the wrong choice.

President Clinton: Secretary of Defense Les Aspin

Management was the scale on which Aspin rated lowest. Great managing skills are not equally in demand in every government department: John Foster Dulles could be an outstanding secretary of state without having ever run anything larger than a corner suite in an elite New York law firm, and Henry Kissinger was a university scholar, not even an academic administrator, before coming to Washington. But you can't survive at the top of the Pentagon with the poor management abilities of a Les Aspin.

The problem, in part, was Bill Clinton's, as Bob Woodward pointed out in the *Washington Post:* "With no military service, and no Washington or national security policymaking experience, Clinton has come into office as perhaps the least experienced commander-in-chief in more than 60 years." So when Clinton reached out to the chairman of the House Armed Services Committee, it might have seemed like a good choice.

But if Clinton had known Aspin—or had deeply inquired about him—he would have discovered that underneath the expertise was a ruminating intellectual, fascinated with arcane questions, undisciplined, really more the absent-minded professor than focused executive expected to run an incredibly complex, multibillion-dollar enterprise. Even if he had not been wrong on some of the major problems that faced the president, Aspin should have been marked as a bad choice to be secretary of defense.

President George W. Bush: Secretary of the Treasury Paul O'Neill

This one is even easier. Paul O'Neill met with Bush and Cheney during the transition and outlined for them all the reasons he should not be appointed secretary of the treasury. Some of the reasons were that he simply didn't agree with them. His blunt style, regardless of his opinions, would be a liability in media-saturated Washington. And, strangely most important, after twelve years of running Alcoa, he didn't think he could be on somebody's staff. And even the secretary of the treasury is ultimately a staffer. They would not believe him.

Part of the reason, one can assume, was because Dick Cheney knew him and admired him when they were both in the Ford administration. But that had been a quarter century earlier. What is so stunning about this mistake is how totally self-inflicted it was.

Make several copies of the following personnel selection form and use them to assess the qualifications of your choices for cabinet-level positions:

Personnel Selection Form

2008 Transition

OFFICE: _____

CANDIDATE: _____

CAREER SUMMARY:

_____
_____
_____
_____
_____

ASSESSMENT:

Management

_____
_____

Expertise

_____
_____

Political Skills

_____
_____

Loyalty

_____

Personal

_____

DECISION: _____

"Résumés over there"
Cartoon by Tom Cheney, ©*The New Yorker*

Beyond the Outer Cabinet

Many of your key appointments, some of which are more important than secretaryship of an outer cabinet department, will be in jobs that have a fixed term, such as the FBI director. Watch their expiration dates carefully. This can be as significant as knowing the date on a can of salmon. The Federal Reserve Board, for example, has seven members, but three positions are vacant at present, and another member's term expires in January 2009. Thus, concludes the *Wall Street Journal* (May 29, 2008), "the next president could have a rare opportunity to redraw the Federal Reserve's leadership . . . quickly putting fingerprints on regulatory policy." Following are some important chair positions, with their current officeholders. These appointments are subject to Senate confirmation.

Plum Jobs

The Plum Book

"The Plum Book" is the name commonly given to a congressional report, "United States Government Policy and Supporting Positions," published just after every presidential election, which lists over 7,000 jobs in the legislative and executive branches of the federal government that may be subject to noncompetitive appointment. Many people seeking positions in the new administration start by checking here to see what is available. In 2008 it will be prepared by the U.S. Office of Personnel Management (OPM) and published by the Senate Committee on Government Reform. Check OPM's website at www.opm.gov.

The Prune Book

After every presidential election, the Council for Excellence in Government publishes a book aimed at those who may wish to join the incoming administration at a relatively high level—"prunes," according to the authors, are "plums seasoned by wisdom and experience, with a much thicker skin." Each volume is different. Past editions have included "The 60 Toughest Science and Technology Jobs" and "The 45 Toughest Financial Management Jobs." The 2008–09 edition—the first to be published online—will highlight "the 25 toughest subcabinet management positions" in the federal government. See www.excelgov.org.

Fixed-Term Appointments

Securities and Exchange Commission
Christopher Cox, Chairman
5-year term, expires 2010

National Labor Relations Board
Peter C. Schaumber, Chairman
2-year term, expires 2010

Federal Communications Commission
Kevin J. Martin, Chairman
5-year term, expires 2011

Surgeon General
Vacant
4-year term

Export-Import Bank
James H. Lambright, Chairman
3-year term, expires 2009

Equal Employment Opportunity Commission
Naomi C. Earp, Chair
5-year term, expires 2010

Nuclear Regulatory Commission
Dale E. Klein, Chairman
5-year term, expires 2011

Federal Bureau of Investigation
Robert Mueller, Director
10-year term, expires 2011
(can be fired)

Federal Deposit Insurance Corp.
Sheila C. Bair, Chair
5-year term, expires 2011

Joint Chiefs of Staff
Mike Mullen, Chairman
2-year term, expires 2009

Activities

So much to do and so little time! Once you deal with the first imperative, which is to concentrate on the White House and cabinet (the biggest pieces in the puzzle of putting together a government), many other matters will demand your attention. But how to handle them all? What about these transition teams that you are being urged to send into the departments? Can they help or hinder you in pinpointing what is necessary to turn campaign promises into the reality of draft legislation and executive orders? Then there is a meeting with the president at the White House to prepare for, meetings with the media (stumbling blocks for many a previous president-elect), and overtures to the civil service. These are among the "activities" you will be fully engaged in right up to the inauguration.

Facing page: John T. McCutcheon, *Chicago Tribune*, 1912?

CHAPTER 4

Activities

Transition Teams

Past presidents-elect have picked teams of supporters to go into the executive departments and report on what they think the new executive should know. The transition teams produce briefing papers that will be passed along to the people you will eventually appoint to cabinet and subcabinet positions.

These temporary jobs will be in great demand. Moreover, taxpayer money is available for authorized transition costs, so they can even be paid jobs—perfect for campaign workers who need to be tided over until you can put them on the permanent payroll. Some supporters,

"My son, you have survived the ordeal by fire and the ordeal by water. You now face the final challenge—ordeal by media."
Cartoon by Lee Lorenz, ©*The New Yorker*

particularly lobbyists, will not aspire to be on the government payroll but will still want some type of recognition. Assigning them to transition teams is a way of providing this recognition on the cheap. Since your predecessors have done this, what can be wrong with following their precedent?

Plenty!

Ask those who have had to contend with the havoc such teams have created for them—the self-important leaks to the media, the time-consuming meetings, the wires crossed in the departments that had to be uncrossed when the designated cabinet officers arrived, some reports with the superficiality of campaign handouts.

Commenting on the 1,500-person Reagan transition of 1980, C. Boyden Gray—who would serve as legal counsel to George H. W. Bush's transition—called the teams a "waste of time and money." Richard Darman, an executive director of Reagan's transition, later said, "If there has been a more colossal waste, I'm not aware of it." And this was the best use of transition teams, according to transition expert Richard Neustadt, who concluded that the teams "get in the way of serious preparation for governing."

Simple Cost-Benefit Analysis for Transition Teams

Transition teams can generate POLITICAL REWARDS *by creating short-term plum jobs for loyalists. Transition teams also incur* POLITICAL COSTS, *in terms of expended energy, demands on your key assistants, leaks, and media distractions. When the costs exceed the* REWARDS, *avoid appointing transition teams.*

The rule: THE COSTS ALMOST ALWAYS EXCEED THE REWARDS.

Task Forces

Task forces are quite another matter. Are we splitting hairs?

No, the differences between transition teams and task forces have to do with size, expertise, and assignment. Instead of blockbuster mandates ("Go figure out what the Interior Department is doing!"), task forces deal with relatively narrow questions that require very specific solutions.

In 1992, for instance, President-elect Bill Clinton selected William A. Galston to chair two separate task forces to examine how he could quickly honor campaign promises to establish a new national service program and to reform student loan programs. Galston's explanation of his student-loan assignment is revealing on at least two fronts—the focus on a specific problem to be solved, and the quickness with which the work of the task force led to legislative action:

> During the campaign, Clinton had offered two different proposals to reform the federal student loan program. One was to establish a new system of direct lending from the federal government to students, bypassing state-level and private-sector intermediaries. The other was to allow students to pay their loans back, not on fixed terms, but rather as a percentage of their earnings over time. Our mission was to figure out how to redeem these two promises, which we did with the assistance of highly knowledgeable experts.

The outcome, Galston continued, was that "the direct lending proposal triggered a memorable battle in the Senate, which lasted all summer and was only resolved with a compromise that allowed a substantial portion of the old system to survive in parallel with the new one."

Consider Setting up a Task Force

☞ *When you need specific policy options to solve a narrowly focused problem.*

☞ *When you need the proposals soon.*

Reorganizations

You are about to be besieged by reports offering ways to reorganize parts—or even all—of the government. Some suggestions will come from task forces you have set in motion. Others will come from well-meaning and deeply experienced outsiders. There will be calls for centralizing and calls for decentralizing, for creating new offices and positions and for abolishing old offices and positions. Some of the ideas will be good ones and will deserve the most serious consideration; some will deserve to be ignored completely. If you have a magic wand to distinguish the two—wave it.

But always keep this thought in mind: reorganizations come with costs. And not merely the cost of printing new stationery when you change the name of an agency, but real political costs. Congressional committees oversee executive agencies *as they currently exist* and may not respond kindly to plans that might move matters out of their jurisdiction. Changes within agencies create confusion for the workers, if not outright hostility. Losing organizational fights—which Main Street usually does not care about anyway—will be a black mark in the ledger the media keep on you.

Of course, some things will need to be changed. What to do?

Start with this wise counsel that outgoing President Eisenhower gave to incoming President Kennedy at the White House on December 6, 1960: *"Avoid any reorganization until you become well acquainted with the problem."*

Eisenhower clearly thought this was advice worth emphasizing: he himself provided the italics when he recounted his discussion with Kennedy in his memoirs.

If You Decide a Reorganization Is Necessary

☞ *Always begin with the changes that are easiest to accomplish.*

☞ *Don't ask for a constitutional amendment if what you want to accomplish can be done by legislation.*

☞ *Don't ask for legislation if what you want to accomplish can be done by executive order.*

☞ *Don't issue an executive order if what you want can be accomplished with a handshake.*

The Reinventing Government Project

You may wish to make the vice president your reorganization specialist.

That is what President Clinton did in 1993, when he put Vice President Al Gore in charge of an interagency task force to determine the challenges that federal employees faced on the job and to make recommendations to improve services, reduce the workforce, and set customer service standards. It later concentrated on agencies with a high degree of interaction with the public, such as the National Park Service and the Internal Revenue Service. On the basis of the task force's recommendations, Congress adopted savings of about $136 billion and reduced the size of the federal workforce by 17 percent. In May 2000 testimony before a Senate committee, public administration expert Donald F. Kettl, now a professor at the University of Pennsylvania, gave the Gore operation an overall grade of "B," saying there was "room for improvement."

Pick a Presidential Portrait

Abraham Lincoln by George Henry Story (1835–1922)
Hung in the Oval Office during the presidency of George W. Bush.

The Contrariness Principle

George W. Bush did not make Bill Clinton's mistakes, and you will not make George W. Bush's mistakes. Each president has a mandate to be different. Although the drive to be different is clearest when there is a change of party, it can happen even when the president's successor is the vice president. The principle of contrariness—the desire to do things differently than your predecessor did—is that strong.

Consider these contrary actions:

☞ *Newly inaugurated President Kennedy disbanded President Eisenhower's National Security Council staff and consequently was left without a properly functioning advisory body in the White House during the Bay of Pigs crisis.*

☞ *Newly installed President Carter wanted to tear down the so-called Berlin Wall that characterized Nixon's White House under chief of staff Bob Haldeman and policy adviser John Ehrlichman. Deciding to have no chief of staff, Carter initially performed tasks that should have been handled by subordinates.*

☞ *Newly installed President Clinton's choice of Thomas "Mack" McLarty as chief of staff is a contrary action if viewed as a response to the sharp-edged management of John Sununu in the George H. W. Bush White House.*

In the rush to change, it takes courage to guard against taking actions simply because of their provenance. A case in point is George W. Bush's vigorous record of attempting to expand—he would say *restore*—presidential powers, many of which related to prosecuting the war on terrorism. You will have to consider these carefully along the security-civil rights axis. But other actions grew out of his reaction to the chipping away of powers—once hailed as Rooseveltian—in the wake of Vietnam, Watergate, and President Clinton's personal scandals.

In the tug-of-war of between Articles I and II of the Constitution—Congress up, President down; President up, Congress down—these are delicate days. Weigh carefully your—and future presidents'—institutional interest in preserving executive power.

The White House Meeting

You are going to have the obligatory session with the president in the Oval Office. Your spouses, perhaps, will go off to tour the residence. Is this meeting just a courtesy call—or is it something more?

A good question.

Outgoing President Herbert Hoover wanted incoming President Franklin D. Roosevelt to jointly deal with the nation's banking crisis; Roosevelt refused, knowing that he would soon have the power to work out his own solution. Outgoing President Lyndon Johnson wanted to call Congress into special session to consider the Nuclear Non-Proliferation Treaty; incoming President Richard Nixon preferred to deal with the issue on his own terms.

There was a very different sort of interaction between the outgoing and incoming presidents in 1980. President Jimmy Carter was engaged in delicate negotiations for the release of American hostages in Iran. President-elect Ronald Reagan wanted the negotiations to be concluded by the time he took office and let it be known that the Iranians would not get a better deal from him. The hostages were released moments after Reagan took the oath of office on January 20, 1981.

Between his defeat in November 1992 and leaving office the following January, President George H. W. Bush sent troops to Somalia in a humanitarian effort to relieve the suffering caused by the country's civil war. Bush sought and received the support of President-elect Bill Clinton. According to Clinton's memoirs, "Bush's national security advisor, General Brent Scowcroft, had told [Clinton aide] Sandy Berger they would be home before my inauguration." But that was not to be. Eighteen Army Rangers were killed in the Battle of Mogadishu on October 3–4, 1993, and a few days later Clinton declared that all U.S. troops would be withdrawn by March 31, 1994. "The battle of Mogadishu haunted me," Clinton wrote. "I thought I knew how President Kennedy felt after the Bay of Pigs."

Preparing for Your Meeting with the President

☞ *Have your staff "game-play" what the president will want from you and possible responses.*

☞ *Compile a list of questions to ask the president. Do you want his assessment of world leaders, friends, and foes? Of areas of government that work well, need improvement, should be scrapped? Best use of the cabinet? Lessons from National Security arrangements? While you may view these as courtesy questions, his answers may surprise you!*

☞ *After you have had your one-on-one session, what others should be invited in? National security team? The economics team?*

☞ *Are there matters for which you may wish to request the president's future involvement?*

☞ *The White House press corps will expect a statement of how useful the meeting has been.*

Reaching Out to Your Government

To incoming President Franklin D. Roosevelt, the permanent employees of the federal government—the bureaucrats he was charged by the Constitution to lead—were a bunch of entrenched conservatives. To incoming President Richard Nixon, they were akin to a branch office of Moscow on the Potomac. It is expected that you will engage in some early stroking of the civil service: perhaps a message, perhaps a day of assemblies among the various departments. But after years of hearing the candidates of both parties campaign against "the mess in Washington," a few nice words are not likely to have a strong impact.

Part of the reason the effort will be unheeded is that neither you nor your cabinet officials are going to have much to do with most government employees. This is how it works inside a government agency: most of the interaction between your political government and the permanent government takes place between high-ranking civil servants and your subcabinet (usually at the deputy assistant secretary level). Based on the quality of your subcabinet officials—their style and generosity, how articulate they are at explaining your policies, how well they listen, the way they seek information and advice—the word will go out, and down, to the rest of government.

Two groups of civil servants are a must to have on your team: the senior executives and Grade 15's.

The Senior Executive Service

This is a unique personnel system that includes most of the top managerial, supervisory, and policy positions in the executive branch that are not required to be filled by presidential appointment and confirmed by the Senate. In 2008, senior executive service salaries ranged from $114,468 to $158,500.

Grade 15 of the General Schedule

This is the highest level of the system that employs most government workers. There are ten salary steps at each grade. The maximum pay in 2008 at the highest GS-15 step was $124,010.

Here's my advice: put away the shotgun for spraying your rhetorical praise over the federal government and take careful aim at these key members of the permanent government. Set up small meetings. Assume that they want to help. Assume that they know a lot more than your appointees about the substance of federal programs. Advise your appointees to listen carefully to what they are being told about how power flows within a department, between agencies, and between the agencies and the congressional committees that have oversight responsibility for them.

If this does not improve government, you can always revive President-elect George H. W. Bush's address to an audience of senior bureaucrats in which he praised them as "unsung heroes."

Getting Good Press, Avoiding Bad Press

In the beginning you will have to work hard to get bad press. Even the unloved Nixon got favorable press at first—in part by cleverly unveiling his entire cabinet at one time on television. Nor did it hurt that Nixon's transition headquarters was located on bustling Fifth Avenue in New York City.

Poor Bill Clinton: Little Rock was not a place to amuse a bored national press corps. But the real problem was the absence of hard news. So the reporters stared at the walls of their rooms in the Capitol Hotel and wrote stories like this by Susan Bennett of the *Philadelphia Inquirer:* "Thanks to snippets of video and a few remarks on the run, it is known that President-elect Clinton likes a morning jog and weekend golf. What is not known after more than thirty days of the transition is anything of substance." No appointments were announced until the transition's sixth week.

The transition press corps is a curious hybrid of campaign reporters and White House regulars. The campaign reporters may feel they know *you* but not the presidency, while the White House regulars may know the *presidency* but not you. They arrive with a healthy curiosity—and perhaps even a little goodwill.

Cartoon by Herblock, following Nixon's election in 1968, courtesy of the Herbert Block Foundation

But the so-called honeymoon period is not really reporters trying to be nice. In fact, it has nothing to do with niceness. Rather, it's the conjunction of two definitions of "good news" at the start of any presidency. Good news for journalists means fresh and interesting stories, while good news for presidents means favorable stories. New people and new policies usually add up to fresh and interesting stories, which hence tend to be favorable.

The trick, of course, is to "feed the beast," as they say in the White House press corps. Give reporters "a constant supply of doggie biscuits," claimed the press secretary of former senator and Clinton treasury secretary Lloyd Bentsen, and they will "gleefully lick the hand that fed them." Run out of treats, and they will "devour your arm."

So what should your press office do when you are behind closed doors deliberating on your choice of cabinet officials?

☞ *Manufacture news.* *An experienced press operation—which at that time did not describe Clinton's youthful team of George Stephanopoulos and Dee Dee Myers—would have followed the example of President Eisenhower's press secretary, Jim Hagerty, who produced a continual stream of "news"—events, meetings, reports—even as the president himself was recovering from a heart attack.*

☞ *Bring in the experts.* *If there are to be long pauses between announcements, have your press team engage reporters on the issues that you will be confronting in the next four years. Use policy experts to put on daily briefings on economic, diplomatic, military, scientific, geographic, demographic, and social policy. An educated press corps can't be all bad.*

Holding Press Conferences

You may have trouble making the adjustment from being covered by the campaign press corps to the White House press corps. Bill Clinton did. Less than two months after taking office he told the White House regulars, "I can stiff you," talk show host Larry King recounted in his book *Anything Goes* (Grand Central, 2000), because "Larry King liberated me by giving me to the American people directly."

But the fact of the matter is that you are not going to appear on Larry King—or Bill O'Reilly or Keith Olbermann—every night. You are going to appear on the evening news programs and in tomorrow morning's headlines. And these stories are produced by sixty or so reporters at the daily press briefings. And you'll need to prepare for sudden shifts in who's reporting: News organizations often reassign reporters when a presidential administration changes. Continuing turbulence in the media industry may also reduce the number of reporters assigned to the expensive White House beat.

An excellent way for you to try to control the flow of information in your first year is to hold frequent, full-dress, televised press conferences.

This is exactly what the White House press corps says it wants—and this is exactly what many of your predecessors have been eager to avoid.

The press conference has a mythical reputation as a breathtaking contest between reporters and the president. Columnist William Rusher once called them "metaphorical bullfights. The president is the bull. The excitement stems from the tension over which of the major protagonists will triumph—the bull or the matador." While Rusher's characterization may be more exaggeration than truth, it is in your interest not to disturb this impression.

First, you can exert considerable control over the press conference with your opening statement, with scripted answers to expected questions, the occasional plant of a question with a friendly reporter, as well as your skill with a Kennedyesque quip, or a deliberately confusing response in the manner of Eisenhower. Or you can simply decline to answer on the grounds of national security.

Second, don't be intimidated. Questioners often *sound* confrontational, and their questions often *sound* tough. (For the journalists, this is good for business and their egos.) But deconstruct the transcripts and you will see how easily you can parry what is coming. You would have to look long and hard to find an instance of a clever questioner forcing a president to reveal information that he wanted to keep to himself. And while it is true that you could seriously misspeak, this has happened only once in the history of presidential press conferences (when Truman implied that the atomic bomb might be used against China during the Korean War).

Finally, hold *frequent* press conferences. What is "frequent?" President George W. Bush has averaged only about six a year. If you hold one press conference every other week (twenty-six a year), you will be hailed in the media for having restored "a critically important means of communication." Moreover, holding frequent press conferences almost guarantees that you will rarely be surprised—because most of the questions will be about things that have happened in the two weeks since you last faced the press.

Preparing for the press takes time, always a scarce commodity. But you should make frequent press conferences an important part of your

2008 White House Press Corps

CNN Ed Henry Elaine Quijano Suzanne Malveaux	**Reuters** Caren Bohan Tabassum Zakaria	**ABC** Martha Raddatz John Hendren
AP Radio Mark Smith	**New York Times** Steven Lee Myers Sheryl Gay Stolberg	**Washington Post** Michael Abramowitz Dan Eggen
ABC News Radio Ann Compton	**National Public Radio** Don Gonyea David Greene	**Washington Times** Jon Ward
Hearst Newspapers	**Voice of America** Scott Stearns Paula Wolfson	**Newsday** Craig Gordon
Houston Chronicle Julie Mason	**FOX Radio** Rich Johnson	**Salem Radio Network** Greg Clugston
Dow Jones Henry J. Pulizzi	**Scripps Howard News Service** Ann McFeatters	**Baltimore Sun** David Nitkin
Washington Examiner	**BNA** Nancy Ognanovich	**New York Post** Charles Hurt

Sources: Julie Mason, *Houston Chronicle,* Mark Knoller, CBS Radio.

PODIUM

Helen Thomas

CBS
Bill Plante
Jim Axelrod

Associated Press
Terry Hunt
Ben Feller
Jennifer Loven
Deb Riechmann

NBC
David Gregory
John Yang

FOX News
Bret Baier
Wendell Goler
Mike Emanuel

Bloomberg
Edwin Chen
Roger Runningen

CBS Radio
Mark Knoller
Peter Maer

Wall Street Journal
John D. McKinnon

Los Angeles Times
James Gerstenzang

Cox News Service
Ken Herman

USA Today
David Jackson

Agence France-Presse
Olivier Knox
Laurent Lozano

Chicago Tribune
Mark Silva

McClatchy
William Douglas
David Lightman

National Journal
Alexis Simendinger

American Urban Radio Networks
April Ryan

CCH
Paula Cruickshank

U.S. News
Kenneth T. Walsh

Time
Massimo Calabresi

Newsweek
Holly Bailey
Richard Wolffe

Media News

Boston Globe

UPI
Marie Horrigan

Politico
Mike Allen

New York Daily News
Kenneth R. Bazinet

San Diego Union-Tribune
George E. Condon Jr.
Finlay Lewis

Dallas Morning News
Todd J. Gillman

Christian Science Monitor
Linda Feldman

strategy of getting your presidency off to a fast start. Just as the public is forming its indelible image of you as president, you'll be stepping into the bullring.

Press Conference Tips

☞ *Your press officers should be able to accurately predict 95 percent of the questions you will be asked. If they can't, make changes!*

☞ *Your chief of staff must be sure that you have the facts and data to back up your answers to expected questions.*

☞ *Don't avoid tough questions. They make for better answers. (If you're prepared.)*

☞ *Count on your press secretary, who runs the morning gaggle and the daily briefing, to alert you to what's going on with "the regulars" (marriages, births, even bad news).*

☞ *Although they are not usually "regulars," call on foreign correspondents and regional reporters from time to time. It will pay dividends.*

Living with Leaks

Leaks, said President Ford in an extraordinary understatement, are a "real pain." Even life in the Senate can't prepare you for the high-level attention they will command within your White House. While preparing yourself for life at the top of a leaky government, it is useful to understand who the leakers are and what steps you might take to keep leaks from causing too many distractions.

If you are like your predecessors, you will first blame leaks on the bureaucrats. But it is a rare bureaucrat who engages in leaking. The civil servants' world faces inward. They know how to work within their own agency to thwart you. In contrast, most journalists are outside their ken and represent risk beyond possible gain. You may next choose to blame press offices. But press offices try to avoid a practice that antagonizes the reporters who do not receive the leaks.

And then you realize: the leakers are your own people—your appointees. *New York Times* columnist James Reston used to say that the ship of state is the only vessel that leaks from the top.

President Carter was right. There is no "effective way to deal with the situation." Attempts to stop leakers—which might involve wiretaps and lie detectors—are always painful, sometimes illegal, rarely successful, and inevitably receive bad press.

So what to do?

☞ *Keep the classification of documents within reasonable bounds.*

☞ *Do not tempt journalists by stamping "secret" on a document unless the purpose is to get something in the media.*

☞ *Be prepared to make a case with editors not to publish some documents.*

☞ *Use cabinet and staff meetings to remind high-level appointees of their obligations not to discuss sensitive information with members of the press.*

☞ *Consider personality as a factor in making top appointments: rivals within your own administration, working at cross-purposes, will be destined to produce leaks.*

☞ *Finally, keep in mind these wise words of Nixon's secretary of state, Henry Kissinger: "Most of the leaks—if you are philosophical about it—go away. I mean, they're unpleasant, but so what? If you ignore them, most of them are not of that huge significance."*

Tales out of School

When I was on the White House staff in the closing years of the Eisenhower presidency, we had an informal rule: the President has the right to tell his story first—then the staff can pile on. The one exception, in our collective opinion, was that Chief of Staff Sherman Adams, who was driven out of government following a scandal, should have the right to defend himself in book form. Eisenhower left office on January 20, 1961; his memoirs were published in 1963. Robert Gray, the secretary to the cabinet, broke our rule when his *Eighteen Acres under Glass* (Doubleday) was published in 1962. Even though it was an innocuous "insider" book, we were incensed by what we considered discourtesy to the president.

Why Leakers Leak

The Ego Leak

Giving information primarily to satisfy a sense of self-importance: in effect, "I am important because I can give you information that is important." This type of leak is popular with staff, who have fewer outlets for ego tripping. Assistants like to tell (and embellish) tales of struggle among their superiors. I believe ego is the most frequent cause of leaking, although it may not account for the major leaks. Other Washington observers disagree. Many reporters and officials prefer to think of leaks as more manipulative and mysterious, but this, of course, also serves their egos.

The Goodwill Leak

A play for a future favor: the primary purpose is to accumulate credit with a reporter, which the leaker hopes can be spent at a later date. This type of leak is often on a subject with which the leaker has little or no personal involvement and happens because most players in governmental Washington gather a great deal of extraneous information in the course of their business and social lives.

The Policy Leak

A straightforward pitch for or against a proposal using some document or insider's information as the lure to get more attention than might be otherwise justified. The great leaks, such as the Pentagon papers in 1971, often fit in this category.

The most critical book by a former Eisenhower staffer, Emmet John Hughes's *Ordeal of Power* (Atheneum), came out in 1963. According to Texas A&M professor Martin Medhurst, "When JFK read the book, he was appalled that someone with such access could display such disloyalty to his principal. He ordered that no one on his staff was ever to produce such an exposé once his administration left office. No one did."

The Animus Leak

Used to settle grudges. Information is disclosed to embarrass another person.

The Trial-Balloon Leak

Revealing a proposal that is under consideration in order to assess its assets and liabilities. Usually proponents have too much invested in a proposal to want to leave it to the vagaries of the press and public opinion. More likely, those who send up a trial balloon want to see it shot down, and because it is easier to generate opposition to almost anything than it is to build support, this is the most likely effect.

The Whistle-Blower Leak

Unlike the others, usually employed by career personnel. Going to the press may be the last resort of frustrated civil servants who feel they cannot correct a perceived wrong through regular government channels. Whistle-blowing is not synonymous with leaking; some whistle-blowers are willing to state their case in public.

Leaks can be meant to serve more than one purpose, which complicates attempts to explain the motivation behind a particular leak. An ego leak and a goodwill leak need not be mutually exclusive; a policy leak also could work as an animus leak, especially since people on each side of a grudge tend to divide along policy lines; and all leaks can have policy implications regardless of motive.

Source: Adapted from Stephen Hess, *The Government/Press Connection: Press Officers and Their Offices* (Brookings, 1984).

For Jimmy Carter the tales-out-of-school came when James Fallows left the White House to become Washington editor of the *Atlantic* and wrote "The Passionless Presidency" for that magazine (May 1979). In the *New York Times,* under the four-column headline "Ex-Speech Writer Views Carter as 'Arrogant, Complacent and Insecure,'" the UPI story began, "James Fallows, President Carter's former chief speech writer, says that Mr. Carter took office 'in profound ignorance' of his job and had made matters worse 'by a combination of arrogance, complacency and insecurity.'" Fallows's assessment included "insider gossip," such as naming the cabinet members that "the White House inner circle 'detest[s].'" According to *Time,* Fallows "seems to have been surprised when the press publicized the nastiest quotes from his piece" and said his article "had been misinterpreted."

Other less-than-flattering accounts of presidents written by insiders while their presidents were still in office (who had not been fired or resigned in protest) include Clinton communications director George Stephanopoulos's *All Too Human* (Little, Brown, 1999) and George W. Bush press secretary Scott McClellan's *What Happened: Inside the Bush White House and Washington's Culture of Deception* (Public Affairs, 2008).

Lessons to Apply to Your Transition

☞ *Make clear to your appointees that they are not there to be historians-in-residence or future journalists.*

☞ *Frank and open discussion is not possible if participants are taking notes for their memoirs.*

☞ *Insider accounts published while you are president will be viewed as intolerable behavior.*

Getting Rid of Deadwood

If you are like most presidents before you, you will be notoriously bad at firing people. This inability is almost a presidential trait. But a year from now you will know whom you should not have hired in the first place.

In some cases you will have to fire someone because a dereliction of public trust is involved or because you need to send a warning to other appointees. In most cases, however, you will simply want the sacked appointee to go away as quietly as possible, without making a fuss.

The easiest way to remove someone is to offer him or her another position. This assumes that the unwanted person is not untalented, but merely in the wrong place. To find the right place involves the fine art of equivalency, balancing the prestige of two different positions.

The master at playing equivalency was President Lyndon Johnson. To remove Robert McNamara as defense secretary, Johnson offered McNamara the presidency of the World Bank. (McNamara accepted.) For Health, Education, and Welfare Secretary Anthony Celebrezze, LBJ dangled a federal judgeship at the U.S. Court of Appeals. (A district court appointment would have been too low.) For Postmaster General John Gronouski, the first Polish American to serve in a president's cabinet, what could be better than getting appointed U.S. ambassador to Poland? (It is an added plus for the president if the new job is out of Washington.)

Other presidents paid a price for not understanding how equivalency works. If President Reagan had offered his chief of staff, Donald Regan, an appointment such as ambassador extraordinary and plenipotentiary to the Court of St. James's, perhaps the fired Regan would not have written a destructive best seller about life in the Reagan White House while Reagan was still living there. Reagan's predecessor, Jimmy Carter, had no aptitude for firing people nicely, as when he abruptly asked for the resignations of five cabinet officers in July 1979 after concluding there was a "crisis of confidence" among the American people.

Assuming you can skillfully remove appointees you come to consider deadwood, there is more good news: you will know *what* you want. You may even know *whom* you want. Given a second chance, the historical odds are great that you will pick the right person. After President Eisenhower cut loose Labor Secretary Martin Durkin, he turned to labor-management specialist James Mitchell, a choice that was even hailed at the AFL-CIO. President Johnson's replacement at Health, Education, and Welfare was John W. Gardner, who became the architect of Johnson's Great Society program. President Nixon was delighted with his new treasury secretary, John B. Connally, after finding an equivalency for Chicago banker David M. Kennedy. (Kennedy became ambassador-at-large, negotiating trade matters around the world.) President Clinton's second defense secretary, William Perry, rates high on the lists of those who make their living ranking defense secretaries. In fact, it is difficult to find an occasion in which a president did worse after deliberately making a midterm cabinet correction.

Mea Culpas

You will make mistakes other than just appointing the wrong person to a cabinet position—all presidents do. But not all presidents admit their mistakes and convince us that they understand why something was a mistake. This, of course, can be the biggest mistake of all.

If you make a mistake and quickly issue a heartfelt mea culpa, it is possible that the media and the public will move on to the next story. That should have been the lesson from President John F. Kennedy's public admission that he had made a mistake by ordering the invasion at Cuba's Bay of Pigs. It is possible that with a meaningful mea culpa—and the jailing of a few co-conspirators—President Nixon would have survived Watergate and not had to resign the presidency.

The one exception to the mea culpa rule is President Bill Clinton's affair with Monica Lewinsky. Had the president's relationship with the intern been quickly confessed, the president would have been toast. His presidency was saved by a long stall during which the opposition overplayed its hand.

Here are some examples of how some of your predecessors admitted (or didn't admit) their mistakes:

> ❝ There is an old saying that victory has a hundred fathers and defeat is an orphan. . . . I am the responsible officer of the government and that is quite obvious. ❞

President John F. Kennedy on the Bay of Pigs (April 21, 1961)

> " People have got to know whether or not their President is a crook. Well, I'm not a crook. I've earned everything I've got. "

President Richard Nixon on Watergate (November 17, 1973)

> " First, let me say I take full responsibility for my own actions and for those of my administration. . . . A few months ago I told the American people I did not trade arms for hostages. My heart and my best intentions still tell me that's true, but the facts and the evidence tell me it is not. "

President Ronald Reagan on Iran-Contra (March 4, 1987)

> " Now, I have to go back to work on my State of the Union, and I worked on it until pretty late last night. But I want to say one thing to the American people. I want you to listen to me. I'm going to say this again: I did not have sexual relations with that woman, Miss Lewinsky. I never told anybody to lie, not a single time; never. These allegations are false, and I need to go back to work for the American people. Thank you. "

President Bill Clinton on the Monica Lewinsky affair (January 26, 1998)

Pick a Presidential Portrait

Franklin D. Roosevelt by Elizabeth Shoumatoff (1888–1980)
Hung in the Oval Office during the presidency of Lyndon Johnson.

It's Not All Work!

If by now you feel institutional forces encircling you, it is worth remembering that being president need not be a grim experience. Some presidents have had a very good time. (A lot depends on personality.)

It may be a bit much to think of the White House as a pleasure palace, but I recall President Eisenhower on sunny afternoons in tan sweater, cap, and golf shoes walking through the doors of the Oval Office onto the South Lawn to practice some swings. Not being a golfer, I once asked his Secret Service escort for instruction and was told that Ike used a nine iron to loft a shot over an obstacle and stop dead. (When I returned to the White House staff eight years later, President Nixon decided to replace the Oval Office's cork floor—badly pockmarked by golf shoes—and Nixon's secretary, Rose Mary Woods, asked me for a list of Ike's friends who might like a square as a remembrance.)

Ike was also a great movie fan, and whenever I walked past the White House theater in the East Wing I'd check the cans of film to see what the president had watched last night. One I remember was *Gunfighters of Abilene,* starring Buster Crabbe. Jim Hagerty, the press secretary, told me the president's favorite movie was *Angel in the Outfield,* something to do with a baseball team aided by divine guidance (not to be confused with a later Walt Disney film of nearly the same name).

As president, you can also see movies at Camp David, your weekend retreat in Maryland's Catoctin Mountains. President Eisenhower took British Prime Minister Harold Macmillan there in 1960 to discuss nuclear weapons tests, and they watched *The Mouse That Roared:* the tale of a tiny country that declares war on the United States, figuring that the loss will bring American aid and solve its economic problems; instead the invaders capture our secret bomb and bring peace to the world by threatening its use.

As for other entertainment possibilities, if you'd like to book a musical group or a soloist for a dinner party, just give a call—usually they are delighted to show up. Invite your friends and staff. Oddly, I was there for one of the most thrilling evenings and one of the most disappointing in the history of White House performances.

The disappointing evening first: In September 1959 Nikita Khrushchev became the first Soviet leader to visit the United States. It was a big moment in the cold war. For the White House event we dressed in "white tie" (in the manner of Fred Astaire), while the commissars wore business suits. (Fortunately I found a going-out-of-business store that sold the tails for $19.95, and slightly less than $40 with the dress shirt, collar, and tie.) We climbed the long flight of marble stairs leading up to the gold ballroom with the delicate crystal chandeliers, took our seats, quickly rose as the center doors swung open to admit the Eisenhowers and the Khrushchevs. Now the entertainment: As reported by President Eisenhower in his memoirs, "This evening's program consisted of some robust music by Fred Waring and his Pennsylvanians that our guest seemed to enjoy thoroughly." My notes, however, read, "The Russian entourage sat stone-faced through the tepid choral performance."

(In fairness to music at the Eisenhower White House, on another evening we heard Leonard Bernstein and the New York Philharmonic play a Mozart concerto and Gershwin's "Rhapsody in Blue." My notes that night, however, were more about Secretary of Defense Thomas Gates "suddenly ill three rows in front of us. . . . Another person far more interested in Mr. Gates's health than in the music was Paul Hume, music critic for the *Washington Post*.")

Now the thrilling evening: April 29, 1969. Gather in the East Room to celebrate Duke Ellington's seventieth birthday. Imagine "Sophisticated Lady," "Mood Indigo," "Take the 'A' Train," "I Got It Bad (And That Ain't Good)," and "It Don't Mean a Thing (If It Ain't Got That Swing)" performed by jazz greats Dizzy Gillespie, Gerry Mulligan, Paul Desmond, Billy Taylor, J. J. Johnson, Louie Bellson, Clark Terry, Earl Hines, Marian McPartland, Hank Jones, Milt Hinton, Urbie Green, Jim Hall, Bill Berry, Lou Rawls, Mary Mayo, and Joe Williams. And Richard Nixon plays "Happy Birthday" in the key of G. To which Ellington

A tape recording of the Duke Ellington birthday concert was produced for the Voice of America by Willis Conover. It is available on CD as "Duke Ellington 1969: All-Star White House Tribute" on the Blue Note label. Also see Leonard Garment's *Crazy Rhythm: From Brooklyn and Jazz to Nixon's White House, Watergate, and Beyond* (Da Capo Press, 2001).

improvises "Pat," a song for First Lady Pat Nixon. The excitement of being among the hundred guests: Isn't that Richard Rodgers, Harold Arlen, Cab Calloway, Billy Eckstine, Otto Preminger, Willie "The Lion" Smith, Vice President Spiro Agnew?

At midnight, the President says good night, but urges guests to stay around for a jam session and dancing. The chairs are cleared. Len Garment, White House aide and former Nixon law partner, who once played tenor sax with Woody Herman, and is most responsible for the Ellington tribute, thinks the East Room has been "transformed into the old Cotton Club." The last of us leaves at 2:45 a.m.

So you see: It's not all work.

Please send response to

The Social Secretary

The White House

at your earliest convenience

A Checklist for the President-Elect

✔ Prioritize policy goals. What to start on Day One and what are long-term objectives.

✔ Design White House organizational plan to balance efficiency and creativity with my work habits.

✔ First appointments: White House staff, starting with 5 positions needed to identify, vet, announce, and confirm Cabinet.

COMPLETE WHITE HOUSE STAFF BY THANKSGIVING

✔ Make National Security and Economic appointments in clusters. Special attention to personality factors that can affect close cooperation.

✔ Highlight the message when announcing appointments. Do not leave impression of randomness.

✔ When picking the rest of the Cabinet, consider honorific add-ons for demographic and political purposes.

✔ Stress to nominees that it is unacceptable to write about my presidency while I'm still president.

COMPLETE CABINET BY CHRISTMAS

✔ Appoint transition teams for political reasons, if necessary.

✔ Appoint task forces to move policy commitments.

✔ Schedule meetings with the following:

      Budget Director (review of next fiscal year options)

      Outgoing president

      Congressional leaders

      Cabinet

      Inaugural committees

      Speechwriters (discuss themes for inaugural address)

      White House usher (living arrangements, special needs)

NOMINEES PREPARED FOR CONFIRMATION HEARINGS, JANUARY 3
OATH OF OFFICE, JANUARY 20

The Inauguration

Dress warmly, Mr. President. I still remember my first Inauguration Day in Washington—January 20, 1961. John F. Kennedy would be sworn in as the new president at noon. Snowfall the night before had left eight inches on the ground. The temperature was 22° F when he took the oath of office and, in the words of Michael Kernan in the *Washington Post*, "The cold wind whisked the cheers from the mouths of the crowd."

But even that day was not a record. The temperature was 4° F at Grant's second inauguration in 1873. It was 55° F for Reagan's first inauguration in 1981, the warmest on record. May you too be a lucky president.

| CHAPTER 5 | # The Inauguration |

At the Capitol

The ceremony itself is fairly formulaic (see the list of inaugural events on page 127), but there is still room for individual touches. President Carter shed the usual morning coat and striped pants for a standard business suit. President Reagan moved the ceremony to the Capitol's west front terrace from the traditional East Portico. (So you will now face the Mall and an audience of many thousands.)

Within patriotic limits, you can choose the musical selections. A chorus from Atlanta University sang "The Battle Hymn of the Republic" at Carter's inauguration. The Mormon Tabernacle Choir sang "This Is My Country" for President Nixon. The Marine Band performed Aaron Copland's "Fanfare for the Common Man" at the inauguration of President Clinton. Pick a grand voice for "The Star-Spangled Banner." Past presidents chose the operatic voices of Dorothy Maynor (Eisenhower), Marian Anderson (Kennedy), and Marilyn Horne (Clinton). President Kennedy opened a new vein of creativity by asking Robert Frost to recite a poem; a second poet, Maya Angelou, read for Clinton.

Choosing the "right" clergy will be noted, of course. Kennedy's invocation was delivered by Richard Cardinal Cushing, Archbishop of Boston, a close family friend. Billy Graham was there for Nixon, George H. W. Bush, and Clinton. Almost as difficult as trying to select a cabinet that "looks like America" is trying to arrange a "four faiths" inaugural ceremony, in which your options include Catholic, Protestant (possibly one white,

According to the National Oceanic and Atmospheric Administration, average noontime conditions for January 20 are about 37° F with partly cloudy skies and wind of about 10 miles per hour. There is about a 15 percent chance of precipitation during the inaugural event, but only a 5 percent chance of snow. There is about a 30 percent chance that there will be snow on the ground from a previous snowfall.

Inauguration Day Events

The Joint Committee on Inaugural Ceremonies has overseen the inaugural ceremonies at the U.S. Capital since 1901. The following events are the highlights of the day:

Morning Worship Service

This tradition began in 1933 when Franklin and Eleanor Roosevelt attended a church service at St. John's Episcopal Church across Lafayette Square from the White House.

Procession to the Capitol

The outgoing president and the president-elect ride together from the White House to the Capitol. This has been a tradition, with few exceptions, since Martin Van Buren and Andrew Jackson took the trip in 1837.

Swearing-in of the Vice President

The vice president's swearing-in was held in the Senate chamber, separate from the president's swearing-in, until 1937, when the ceremony was moved to the outside platform. Since World War II, the oath of office has been administered by a person chosen by the vice president.

Swearing-in of the President

The president's oath of office is prescribed by Article II, Section 1, Clause 8 of the Constitution, but the Constitution says nothing about the inaugural ceremony.

Inaugural Address

The tradition of delivering an inaugural address began with George Washington's inauguration on April 30, 1789, in New York City. Only five presidents never gave an inaugural address: John Tyler, Millard Fillmore, Andrew Johnson, Chester Arthur, and Gerald Ford.

Inaugural Luncheon

The luncheon, held in the Capitol's Statuary Hall and hosted by the Joint Congressional Committee on Inaugural Ceremonies, dates back to 1897.

Inaugural Parade

The inaugural parade is a tradition that also began with George Washington's first inauguration. The parade first took place in Washington, D.C., for Thomas Jefferson's inauguration in 1801. Women first participated in 1917, and the first televised parade occurred in 1949.

Inaugural Ball

This tradition began with Dolley Madison's hosting a gala in 1809. Charity balls became the fashion in the 1920s and 1930s. Official balls are now planned by the Presidential Inaugural Committee.

Source: Joint Committee on Inaugural Ceremonies website (inaugural.senate.gov).

one African American), Jewish, and Greek Orthodox. There has not yet been a Muslim.

Immediately before you take the oath of office, your vice president will be sworn in. There is no set protocol for the vice presidential swearing-in. The oath of office was administered to Vice President Lyndon Johnson by his fellow Texan, Speaker of the House Sam Rayburn. Vice President Richard Nixon chose a fellow Californian, Senator William Knowland, and Vice President Dan Quayle chose Supreme Court Justice Sandra Day O'Connor. The oath of office was administered to Vice President Al Gore by retired Justice Thurgood Marshall.

Once this is done, you will join the chief justice of the United States and place your hand on a Bible, opened to a passage if you wish. You

"Okay, bring in the new guy . . . "
Cartoon by Tony Auth, ©2006 *The Philadelphia Inquirer,* used by permission of Universal Press Syndicate. All rights reserved

will then repeat the thirty-five-word oath from Article II, Section I of the Constitution:

I, _____ , do solemnly swear [or affirm] that I will faithfully execute the Office of President of the United States, and will to the best of my ability, preserve, protect and defend the Constitution of the United States.

You will probably also add the words "So help me God," as most of your predecessors have—a tradition that is said to date to the very first presidential inauguration. Franklin Pierce and Herbert Hoover are the only presidents to "affirm" the oath.

Now, for the first time, ruffles and flourishes and "Hail to the Chief" will be played for you. In the distance a twenty-one-gun salute will be fired from howitzers of the Military District of Washington. You will be given the card that unlocks the nuclear code.

Inauguration Ceremony Checklist

Bible(s): _____

Biblical passage(s) (optional): _____

Preferred music: _____

Musicians: _____

Poet (optional): _____

List of clergy to attend (minimum of three faiths):

_____

_____

_____

The Speech

Mr. President, it would be wonderful if you deliver a great inaugural address. But if you don't, take comfort: very few of your predecessors

Capitol Ceremony

President	Oath
Dwight D. Eisenhower (1953)	Chief Justice Frederick Vinson
John F. Kennedy (1961)	Chief Justice Earl Warren
Richard M. Nixon (1969)	Chief Justice Earl Warren
Jimmy Carter (1977)	Chief Justice Warren Burger
Ronald Reagan (1981)	Chief Justice Warren Burger
George H. W. Bush (1989)	Chief Justice William Rehnquist
Bill Clinton (1993)	Chief Justice William Rehnquist
George W. Bush (2001)	Chief Justice William Rehnquist

did. In fact, as the history books often point out, the inaugural address that had the most immediate effect was certainly one of the worst: sixty-eight-year-old William Henry Harrison spoke for nearly two hours (at 8,445 words, also the longest-ever address) on a snowy day in March 1841. He caught cold and died of pneumonia a month later.

William Safire, a former speechwriter for President Nixon and author of *Lend Me Your Ears: Great Speeches in History* (W. W. Norton, 2004), writes that there have been four great inaugural addresses:

The Avalon Project of the Yale Law School is an online collection of important documents in law, history, and diplomacy—including the fifty-four presidential inaugural addresses from George Washington to George W. Bush. See www.yale.edu/lawweb/avalon/presiden/inaug/inaug.htm.

Bible	Attire	Weather
George Washington's Bible (open to Psalm 127:1) and the West Point Bible (open to 2 Chronicles 7:14)	Morning coat, striped pants, black homburg	Cloudy, 49° F
Family Bible (closed)	Morning coat, striped pants, top hat	Sunny, 22° F
Family Bible (open to Isaiah 2:4)	Morning coat, striped pants	Cloudy, 35° F
George Washington's Bible (open to Micah 6:9)	Business suit	Sunny, 28° F
Family Bible (open to 2 Chronicles 7:14)	Morning coat, striped pants	Cloudy, 55° F
George Washington's Bible (open to Matthew 5)	Business suit with silver necktie	Cloudy, 51° F
Family Bible (open to Galatians 6:8)	Business suit with blue necktie	Sunny, 40° F
Family Bible (closed)	Business suit	Rainy, 35° F

Lincoln's two, Franklin D. Roosevelt's first, and John F. Kennedy's. Others make claims for Jefferson's first and Wilson's second.

Lincoln, elected on the eve of the Civil War, wanted to make clear that he was not going to let the South walk away from the Union. He was prepared to fight. Lincoln's second, delivered four years later and thirty-seven days away from the end of the Civil War, was a sermon looking to reconciliation. Franklin D. Roosevelt's speech of March 4, 1933, also came in the midst of exceptional crisis. One out of every four workers was out of a job, and many banks in all forty-eight states were either closed or placed restrictions on how much money depositors could withdraw. Roosevelt's "bold tone and buoyant delivery," Safire writes, "encouraged people parched for hope."

What is so remarkable about Kennedy's speech is that 1961 was no more a moment of crisis than were any of the other inaugural years of the cold war from Truman through Reagan. Rather, what was instantly hailed was the sheer brilliance of the words, the flow of passion celebrating youth and idealism.

Inaugural addresses are not expected to be heavy on specifics, to detail legislative or administrative proposals. That is what your State of the Union message is for. But you can make an exception to this rule, if you choose, as President Truman did in 1949 when he used his inaugural address to outline four points of action for "world recovery and lasting peace." His fourth point—which called for "a bold new program for making the benefits of our scientific advances and industrial progress available for the improvement and growth of underdeveloped areas"— quickly turned into a major U.S. foreign policy initiative.

Nor are inaugural addresses expected to sound like campaign speeches. Again, there are exceptions: Ronald Reagan's first inaugural address repackages the same themes—often using the same words— that he had been honing into a basic message since campaigning for Barry Goldwater in 1964.

As a member in good standing of the Judson Welliver Society, the collectivity of former presidential speechwriters, I offer here some advice to review with your own team of future Welliverians:

The Judson Welliver Society is a social club for former presidential speechwriters of both political parties. Founded by William Safire (Nixon) and Jack Valenti (Johnson), the club takes its name from Judson Welliver, who served Warren Harding and is widely considered the first official presidential speechwriter.

Length

You will not set the record for the shortest inaugural address. George Washington will always hold that one—a mere 135 words. The gold standard is now Kennedy's twelve minutes. If you can stay around twelve minutes, the commentator class will take note with appreciation.

Famous Passages from Inaugural Addresses

In your hands, my dissatisfied fellow-countrymen, and not in mine, is the momentous issue of civil war. The Government will not assail you. You can have no conflict without being yourselves the aggressors. You have no oath registered in heaven to destroy the Government, while I shall have the most solemn one to "preserve, protect, and defend" it.

Abraham Lincoln's First Inaugural Address, March 4, 1861

With malice toward none; with charity for all; with firmness in the right, as God gives us to see the right, let us strive on to finish the work we are in; to bind up the nation's wounds; to care for him who shall have borne the battle, and for his widow, and his orphan—to do all which may achieve and cherish a just and lasting peace, among ourselves, and with all nations.

Abraham Lincoln's Second Inaugural Address, March 4, 1865

This great Nation will endure as it has endured, will revive and will prosper. So, first of all, let me assert my firm belief that the only thing we have to fear is fear itself—nameless, unreasoning, unjustified terror which paralyzes needed efforts to convert retreat into advance.

Franklin D. Roosevelt's First Inaugural Address, March 4, 1933

In the long history of the world, only a few generations have been granted the role of defending freedom in its hour of maximum danger. I do not shrink from this responsibility—I welcome it. I do not believe that any of us would exchange places with any other people or any other generation. The energy, the faith, the devotion which we bring to this endeavor will light our country and all who serve it—and the glow from that fire can truly light the world. And so, my fellow Americans: ask not what your country can do for you— ask what you can do for your country.

John F. Kennedy's Inaugural Address, January 20, 1961

Style

Do not try to be a Kennedy clone. Clinton did—and while there were moments that were quite good in his first inaugural address, do you really want to be thought of as a weak carbon copy of someone else?

Don't worry about creating applause lines for the people facing you on the Mall. They are your devoted supporters; they already love you. Your primary audience is measured in millions, in the United States and abroad, curious for a first impression of the new president and willing to give you a few minutes in the midst of their busy lives. Humor rarely works. A catchphrase might work for Kennedy ("new frontier"), but how many remember which president created "new covenant" and "new spirit"?

Tone

George W. Bush's first inaugural was a great speech—for some other president. Was a Texas "brush-whacker" supposed to sound that elegant? (Apparently he thought so.) Jimmy Carter—who is said to have written his own speech—did well by sounding like Jimmy Carter, even if there were some at the time who were disappointed. Be comfortable with your rhetorical self.

Theme

Refer back to worksheets in the first chapter in which you wrote down why you were elected and what you promised to accomplish as president. If you campaigned for "change" or "reform," this is the moment to put those ideas in the context of how you plan to govern. Ask not what you can cram into twelve minutes, but rather what is the one thought—even the one word—that best describes what you want your presidency to stand for.

Take a moment to look at what your predecessors said on Inauguration Day—and then find the words to make your own speech memorable.

Dwight D. Eisenhower (1953)

Context

The former five-star general, who led the Allies in Europe during World War II, brought the GOP back to the White House for the first time since 1933, with an overwhelming victory over Democrat Adlai Stevenson. The nation was still engaged in fighting the Korean War and, during his transition, Ike kept his campaign promise ("I shall go to Korea") by visiting American forces there in December 1952.

Speech (2,460 words; 21 minutes)

In the forty-eight pages of his prepared text, Eisenhower devoted forty-one of them to foreign affairs. The speech was described by the *Washington Post* as "a fervent plea for free world unity in time of peril" and by W. H. Lawrence in the *New York Times* as promising a ceaseless "quest for an honorable worldwide peace." The president outlined nine "fixed principles" for peace, including expanded regional defense arrangements, making the United Nations an effective force, and encouraging world trade.

Reaction

The speech was interpreted as a clear break with the isolationist policies that had once dominated the Republican Party and was, according to John Norris in the *Washington Post*, "a declaration of continuity of American foreign policy." In fact, concluded James Reston of the *New York Times*, "The first reaction here was that it was not much different from the rhetoric that had poured out of Democratic leaders here and in the United Nations and in other capitals of the Western world during the last year of the Cold War."

continued

John F. Kennedy (1961)

Context

Defeating Vice President Richard Nixon in one of the closest presidential elections in history, Kennedy became America's first Roman Catholic president. The youngest man ever elected president (at age forty-three), Kennedy took over from Dwight Eisenhower, who at the age of seventy was then the oldest president to have occupied the White House.

Speech (1,364 words; 12 minutes)

"Let the word go forth . . . that the torch has been passed to a new generation of Americans—born in this century, tempered by war, disciplined by a hard and bitter peace." In one of the shortest inaugural addresses ever delivered, Kennedy's recurring theme was muscular challenges confronting "the new generation," which was ready to "pay any price, bear any burden, meet any hardship . . . to assure the survival and the success of liberty."

Reaction

The speech was instantly hailed as a great speech, the words "almost Biblical in their simplicity" and "Churchillian," according to Robert Albright in the *Washington Post.* Albright compared the style of the speech to both Lincoln's Gettysburg Address, which also "shied away from long words," and to Franklin Roosevelt's First Inaugural Address:

"The only thing we have to fear is fear itself." (Roosevelt)

"Let us never negotiate out of fear. But let us never fear to negotiate." (Kennedy)

Richard M. Nixon (1969)

Context

In the midst of the long, costly, and increasingly unpopular war in Vietnam, President Johnson declined to seek reelection. His vice president, Hubert Humphrey, narrowly lost the general election to Richard Nixon, who brought to the office a history of razor-sharp partisanship.

Speech (2,124 words; 17 minutes)

Avoiding the major themes of his campaign—law and order and civil disobedience—Nixon asked Americans to "stop shouting at one another." His speech was designed to stress reconciliation, both at home and abroad. "No man can be fully free while his neighbor is not. . . . This means black and white together, as one nation," borrowing a phrase from the civil rights anthem, "We Shall Overcome." In the words of the *Washington Post's* Chalmers Roberts, "There was no note of partisan political triumph."

Reaction

The speech's muted tone was appreciated. Liberal columnist Joseph Kraft noted that the new president emphasized words like "together" and "negotiations." Kraft concluded, "Mr. Nixon, in sum, was speaking in homilies. But he had the right homilies for the moment."

Jimmy Carter (1977)

Context

Losing the support of his party in the wake of the Watergate scandal, Nixon resigned the presidency on August 9, 1974. He was succeeded by his vice president, Gerald Ford, who brought a friendly and easygoing manner to the office. In the general election in 1976, Ford's opponent was a little-known former governor of Georgia, but the Watergate scandal and the legacy of Vietnam were sufficient to depose the Republican and send a Democrat to the White House.

Speech (1,229 words; 15 minutes)

Carter's theme was a restatement of America's traditional ideals. "I have no new dream to set forth today," he said, "but rather urge a fresh faith in the old dream." The tone was sermonic, recalling the Hebrew prophet Micah: "He hath showed thee, O man, what is good; and what doth the Lord require of thee, but to do justly, and to love mercy, and to walk humbly with thy God?"

continued

Reaction

"It was, on balance, a strongly religious speech—too simply pietistic perhaps," concluded *Time.* "But it was also an accurate expression of Carter's faith—a faith shared by a great many Americans." Yet it was not the speech that most engaged Americans. "Most dramatic," wrote Haynes Johnson in the *Washington Post,* was "the sight of the new President strolling down Pennsylvania Avenue hand-in-hand with his wife and [nine-year-old] daughter Amy." There was plenty of symbolism for all as Carter "set out on his own and walked his way to the White House."

Ronald Reagan (1981)

Context

Carter's presidency was tarnished by the Iranian hostage crisis, double-digit inflation, and long lines at the gas pump. The election of former California governor Ronald Reagan completed a conservative re-alignment within the Republican Party that had begun with the 1964 campaign of Barry Goldwater—in which the former actor Reagan first emerged as a national conservative spokesman.

Speech (2,423 words; 20 minutes)

"Government is not the solution to our problem," Reagan said. "Government is the problem." Lou Cannon, a *Washington Post* reporter and later a Reagan biographer, called the speech "a subdued, evocative version of the same basic message which elected him." The speech was also meant to contrast with the outgoing president's "talk of self-sacrifice and a 'national malaise.'"

"We have every right to dream heroic dreams," declared the new president.

Reaction

Iran released the fifty-two American hostages just minutes after Reagan was sworn into office. According to Hedrick Smith in the *New York*

Times, "Almost unavoidably the human drama in Iran overshadowed an Inaugural Address that was less an inspirational call to national greatness than a plain-spoken charter of Mr. Reagan's conservative creed. . . . In political terms, the hostage release enabled Mr. Reagan to enter the White House in a glow of good feeling."

George H. W. Bush (1989)

Context
With the nation celebrating relative peace and prosperity, the electorate did something unusual: it gave one political party three victories in a row. Reagan, after two terms, still had enough of a breeze at his back to sweep his vice president into the White House. In the process, Bush became the first sitting vice president elected to succeed a president since Martin Van Buren in 1837. His inaugural address would have to promise continuity along with change.

Speech (2,320 words; 20½ minutes)
"A nation refreshed by freedom stands ready to push on," wrote David Hoffman in the *Washington Post.* The speech "displayed a low key, almost humble style." "Some see leadership as high drama, and the sound of trumpets calling. And sometimes it is that," Bush said. "But I see history as a book with many pages. . . . Today a chapter begins: a small and stately story of unity, diversity and generosity, shared, and written, together."

Reaction
In a day almost unmarked by protest and dedicated to the pomp and circumstance of the transfer of power, the reaction to the speech was quietly positive. It was nicely written. What most appealed to Washington—which had witnessed many battles between the executive and legislative branches during Reagan's tenure—was the new president's announcement of a "new engagement" with Congress.

continued

Bill Clinton (1993)

Context

After twelve years of one party's occupying the White House, the out-party can usually count on a collection of unmet needs and a general desire for new faces and new energy. But what was most important in propelling the election of Clinton was the poor state of the economy. Aided by gadfly independent candidate Ross Perot, who skimmed votes from the incumbent, Clinton picked a good time to run against Washington and the Republican Party.

Speech (1,598 words; 14 minutes)

Now a generation removed from John Kennedy, another young Democrat—inspired by Kennedy as a teenager—employed some of the same themes of a new generation rising to meet the country's challenges. "A new season of American renewal has begun." "While America rebuilds at home, we will not shrink from the challenges, nor fail to seize the opportunities, of this new world." "There is nothing wrong with America that cannot be cured by what is right with America." *Washington Post* reporter Dan Balz noted that the speech "was short—14 minutes almost to the second—and crisply delivered, with a fresh cadence rarely achieved in his other major speeches." But Kennedy's Inaugural Address is a hard act to follow.

Reaction

The inauguration was less memorable for the address than for the rest of the celebration. Mezzo-soprano Marilyn Horne sang the national anthem. Poet Maya Angelou read one of her verses. The parade featured everyone from gay groups to Elvis impersonators. The crowds along Pennsylvania Avenue chanted "walk, walk!"—and the Clintons got out of their new armor-plated Cadillac to take the last few blocks on foot. One report said there were eleven inaugural balls, another said fourteen. The national reaction to Clinton's inauguration was that Washington was once again going to be a lively place.

George W. Bush (2001)

Context

The winner received 500,000 fewer votes than the loser. George W. Bush became only the fourth president in history—the first since 1888—to win the election despite losing the popular vote. He was the first president whose victory was decided by the Supreme Court, thirty-six days after voters went to the polls, in a 5–4 decision. Bush was also the first son of a former president to become president since 1825.

Speech (1,584 words; 14½ minutes)

The dominant word was "civility." He used it again and again: "Civility is not a tactic or a sentiment. . . . I will live and lead by these principles—to advance my convictions with civility, to pursue the public interest with courage, to speak for greater justice and compassion, to call for responsibility, and try to live it as well." Folksy in manner and never noted for rhetorical skills, Bush chose a text that the *New York Times* described as both "elegant" and "eloquent." His alliterative promise to the nation was to lead with "civility, courage, compassion, and character."

Reaction

When the overwhelming political need was to bring opposing forces closer together in Washington, where the new Senate was divided 50-50, and Republicans held a mere nine-seat majority in the House, a well-received speech whose themes were inclusiveness and compassion was a good beginning, but the new president offered no clues on whether he planned to moderate his conservative agenda.

THE OVAL OFFICE

You are about to move into the Oval Office—one of the most dramatic, architecturally satisfying rooms in the world—and you are going to have to make a basic decision: do you wish to admire it or work in it?

CHAPTER 6

The Oval Office

Room with a View

Clearly, this is a great ceremonial place. You will call in members of the press pool to snap photos of you chatting with world leaders, with the marble mantel of the fireplace in the background, the presidential seal set in plaster on the ceiling, the flags of the United States and the president behind the desk. But is this really where you want to roll up your sleeves, spread out your papers, loosen your tie and work?

I have worked in the White House twice, for two very different people, and their answers were yes (Eisenhower) and no (Nixon). The Oval Office was where President Eisenhower chose to conduct the affairs of state. He didn't even bother to change the green carpet and draperies from Harry Truman's occupancy. Nixon, on the other hand, established his serious workspace across the gated West Executive Street and up a flight of stairs in Room 180 of the Executive Office Building (since renamed the Eisenhower Executive Office Building; see chapter 2). It was here that Nixon probably had a hole drilled into his desk to secure the wires to the machine that was taping "Watergate" conversations. The Oval Office was relegated to the ceremonial place.

The president who made himself most at home in the Oval Office was John F. Kennedy. He brought in a rocking chair to ease his back pain; his collection of ship models; maritime paintings (instead of presidential portraits); a silver goblet from New Ross, Ireland, the town from which his great grand-

> The oval shape of the president's office, according to the White House Historical Association, was inspired by rooms George Washington had remodeled for his formal receptions ("levees") in the president's residence in Philadelphia. When men of prominence—wearing formal dress (silver buckles, powdered hair)—arrived to meet the president, they formed a circle. Washington walked around the circle addressing each guest in turn. He bowed, but never shook hands. See www.whitehousehistory.org.

President Nixon had the Oval Office redecorated in the summer of 1969 while he was vacationing in San Clemente. I was in my ground-floor office in the West Wing when I got a call from Pat Moynihan: Come upstairs to the Oval Office (a request followed by a string of exclamation points).

The door to the Oval Office is open when the president is not there. Pat had been passing by on his way to the swimming pool (soon to be covered over to make extra space for the press corps). What he had to show me was the sudden redecoration: gold draperies under a single gold valance, gold upholstery for sofas and chairs, a royal blue rug with gold presidential seal. This gold was so bright that my eight-year-old son, after visiting the president, complained that the color had hurt his eyes.

But for Pat the greatest offense was the seals on the chair cushions. He picked up the phone outside the Oval Office and asked to be connected to Bob Haldeman in San Clemente. "Bob, I'm standing outside the Oval Office. If you don't do something fast, every member of Congress will soon be farting on the seal of the presidency."

By the time the president returned to Washington, there were fewer decorative seals in the Oval Office. When President Ford promised "our national nightmare is over," this included toning down Nixon's Oval Office décor, the royal blue rug replaced with one of light yellow and the gold draperies replaced by rust-colored ones.

father set off for America; a watercolor of the White House painted by his wife; a chair from his student days at Harvard; and a plaque, given to him by Admiral Hyman Rickover, inscribed with the words of the Breton fisherman's prayer: "O, God, Thy sea is so great and my boat is so small." On his desk, encased in plastic, sat the coconut shell carved with the message that led to his rescue after PT-109 was cut in two by a Japanese destroyer in the Solomon Islands.

Other presidents added their own personal touches. Reagan gave the Oval Office a distinctly Western flavor with Remington cowboy sculptures and miniature bronze saddles. George H. W. Bush featured blue and white, the colors of Yale, his alma mater. His son hung scenes of Texas by Texan artists on loan from Texas museums.

List Personal Items to Keep in the Oval Office

_____

_____

_____

_____

_____

Portraits

You don't have to hang a presidential portrait in the Oval Office (Eisenhower and Kennedy didn't), but if you do, the odds are that it will be Washington. You can choose Washington in military uniform or in civilian clothes. He comes in all sizes. The question, then, is which one? There are portraits of Washington by Charles Willson Peale, by his son Rembrandt Peale, and by Gilbert Stuart.

George Washington

Charles Willson Peale (1741–1827), Philadelphia's leading artist, painted the first seven presidents as well as Benjamin Franklin. (President Ford hung Peale's Franklin portrait in the Oval Office.) Peale traveled to Mount Vernon in 1772 to paint his first portrait from life of Washington. It was a three-quarter-length likeness (from the knees up) in the uniform of a Virginia militia colonel, Washington's rank at the close of the French and Indian War. Peale's next knees-up portrait (50″ x 39″) was painted in 1776. It was commissioned by John Hancock and shows Washington as commander-in-chief of the Continental Army. Washington last sat for Peale in 1795, when the artist brought his sons Raphaelle and Rembrandt to paint the president. In all, Charles Willson Peale painted Washington from life seven times.

Many of the most famous portraits of U.S. presidents are on permanent exhibition at the National Portrait Gallery, part of the Smithsonian Institution, in Washington, D.C. "Portraits of the Presidents" is the National Portrait Gallery's online exhibit, with brief biographies and portraits of presidents from Washington to Clinton. Go to www.npg.si.edu.

George Washington, **by Charles Willson Peale**

This portrait hung in the Oval Office during the presidencies of Nixon, Ford, Carter, and Reagan.

❏ Yes, this is the portrait I would like to hang in the Oval Office.

George Washington, **by Rembrandt Peale**

This portrait hung in the Oval Office during the presidencies of George H. W. Bush, Clinton, and George W. Bush.

❏ Yes, this is the portrait I would like to hang in the Oval Office.

George Washington, **by Gilbert Stuart**

This portrait hung in the Oval Office during the presidencies of Johnson and Nixon.

❏ Yes, this is the portrait I would like to hang in the Oval Office.

Rembrandt Peale (1778–1860) was one of the eleven children of Charles Willson Peale by his first wife. (He had six more children by his second wife.) Rembrandt studied for several years in Paris where he developed a neoclassical style that was distinct from his father's. It was written that "his portraits were distinguished by a much crisper modeling, harder surfaces, and brighter coloring." He painted more than 100 portraits of Washington in a range of sizes.

Gilbert Stuart (1755–1828), America's leading portraitist of the Federal period, spent the Revolutionary War in London (unlike Charles Willson Peale, who fought in the battles of Trenton and Princeton). Stuart returned to America in 1793 and secured his first sitting with

Andrew Jackson, **after Thomas Sully**

Four presidents kept Jackson on the wall during their time in the Oval Office: Nixon, Reagan, George H. W. Bush, and Clinton.

❏ Yes, this is the portrait I would like to hang in the Oval Office.

Abraham Lincoln, **by George Henry Story**

George W. Bush had this portrait in the Oval Office.

❏ Yes, this is the portrait I would like to hang in the Oval Office.

Franklin D. Roosevelt, **by Elizabeth Shoumatoff**

Lyndon B. Johnson had this portrait in the Oval Office.

❏ Yes, this is the portrait I would like to hang in the Oval Office.

Washington in Philadelphia in 1795. He made about twelve copies of this portrait. Martha Washington then commissioned portraits of herself and her husband; they sat for him in 1796, but he never delivered. (The now-famous portraits remained with him until his death.) He was notorious for not finishing commissions. Thomas Jefferson was still waiting for his portrait twenty years after first sitting. One hazard of having done so many Washington portraits is that Stuart spent much time in court fighting unauthorized copying.

If you choose not to hang one of the Washington portraits, there are many other presidential portraits you may consider, including these famous ones of Andrew Jackson, Abraham Lincoln, and Franklin D. Roosevelt.

Andrew Jackson

According to the National Gallery of Art in Washington, this portrait of Andrew Jackson is a replica of a study that Thomas Sully (1783–1872) painted from life in 1824, when Jackson was a U.S. senator and a presidential candidate. The replica was completed shortly before Jackson's death in April 1845.

Four presidents kept Jackson on the wall during their time in the Oval Office: Nixon, Reagan, George H. W. Bush, and Clinton. Strangely, perhaps, given that Jackson was a patron saint of the Democratic Party, three of these Jackson enthusiasts were Republicans.

Abraham Lincoln

George Henry Story (1835–1922), as a young man in Washington in 1860, became a friend of Lincoln's and posed the president for the first official photograph taken in Washington. Story painted several Lincoln portraits. "On three successive days," Story wrote, "I quietly entered the President's office through Secretary Nicolay's room and made pencil notes of my subject and mental observations of the changes in his countenance while he was in real life and under the influence of State affairs in different interviews with his visitors."

George W. Bush had this portrait in the Oval Office as well as a bust of Lincoln by Augustus St. Gaudens. Clinton also had a Lincoln bust, but it was his personal property.

Franklin D. Roosevelt

The only twentieth-century president whose portrait has hung in the Oval Office is Franklin D. Roosevelt, although there have been busts of Truman (George H. W. Bush and Clinton) and Eisenhower (George W. Bush). The Roosevelt portrait, honored by Lyndon Johnson, is the one that FDR was sitting for in his cottage at Warm Springs, Georgia, when he was stricken and died, April 12, 1945. The artist was Elizabeth Shoumatoff (1888–1980). She later painted the official portrait of President Johnson after he angrily rejected one done by Peter Hurd.

You get a second chance to hang presidential portraits in the Cabinet Room, where there is space for up to four. Past selections have tended to be predictable, although Reagan hung Coolidge and Taft

In 1996 I joined a group chosen by Arthur M. Schlesinger Jr. to rate presidents on a scale from "great" to "failure." Nothing scientific; just for fun. The results appeared in the *New York Times Magazine*. Our "greats" were Lincoln, Washington, and Franklin D. Roosevelt. (Lincoln got all thirty-two votes; Washington and FDR each received one "near great" vote—go figure!) Next in order were Jefferson, Jackson, and Theodore Roosevelt. Comparing this list to the portraits picked by presidents to hang in the Oval Office, the only surprises are that Jackson did so well and that no one wanted Jefferson. (Most presidents put him in the Cabinet Room.)

In the far more sophisticated "rating game" of Alvin Stephen Felzenberg, Jefferson and Jackson rank much lower on the measure of presidential greatness. In his 2008 book *The Leaders We Deserved (And a Few We Didn't)* (Basic Books), Felzenberg devised separate categories for character, vision, competence, economic policy, preserving and extending liberty, and defense/foreign policy. Lincoln and Washington still came out on top, but Jefferson (fourteenth of thirty-nine presidents) and Jackson (twenty-seventh) ranked quite low. Perhaps the final word belongs to Schlesinger: "There is force in the argument that only presidents can really understand the presidency."

there. President Johnson made perhaps the oddest choice—James Buchanan.

Desks

In addition to deciding which portraits to hang in the Oval Office, you will have to choose which desk you will use there. The options, however, are limited to four historic desks—the Resolute Desk, the Theodore Roosevelt Desk, the Wilson Desk, and the C&O Desk—or bringing your own.

The Resolute Desk

Its story, as explained by Betty C. Monkman in *The White House: Its Historic Furnishings and First Families* (Abbeville Press, 2000), is that a British ship of that name was sent out in 1852 to search for explorer

Sir John Franklin who was lost on a voyage to discover the Northwest Passage. The Resolute was trapped in ice and abandoned in 1854, discovered and extricated by an American whaler in 1855, refitted with a $40,000 congressional appropriation, and sent back to England as a gift to Queen Victoria. When the Resolute was decommissioned and dismantled in 1879, timber from it was made into a desk as a gift for the president of the United States.

The Resolute Desk is a partner's desk, meaning it was designed to accommodate a person sitting and working on either side. Franklin D. Roosevelt, however, chose to add a center panel with a carved Seal of the President in order to hide his iron leg braces from view and to conceal a safe. While the desk has been used often by presidents since 1880, Kennedy was the first to put it in the Oval Office. Carter, Reagan, Clinton, and George W. Bush also used the Resolute Desk in the Oval Office.

The Resolute Desk

Theodore Roosevelt Desk

This is the original West Wing desk, made in 1902 for Theodore Roosevelt, used in the Oval Office by Taft, Wilson, Harding, Coolidge, Hoover, Franklin D. Roosevelt, Truman, and Eisenhower. Nixon chose this desk for his "working office," Room 180 in the Eisenhower Executive Office Building, and presumably the Watergate tapes were made by an apparatus concealed in its drawer. Its practicality is that it has a larger surface than the Resolute Desk.

The Wilson Desk

The Wilson Desk was used in the Oval Office by Presidents Nixon and Ford. This was Nixon's desk in the Capitol when he was vice president, and he requested it for the White House. His attachment stemmed from his belief that the desk once belonged to Woodrow Wilson. He liked to make Wilsonian points, according to speechwriter William Safire in his book *Before the Fall,* "about how Presidents

The Roosevelt Desk

can be misunderstood, how peaceful men find themselves with need to do battle, how the distinction between men of thought and men of action can no longer be drawn, etc."

Unfortunately, Safire had to tell the president that the desk belonged to a less notable Wilson, causing the following "petulantly accurate" footnote in the 1969 edition of *Public Papers of the Presidents:* "Later research indicated that the desk had not been President Woodrow Wilson's as had long been assumed but was used by Vice President Henry Wilson during President Grant's administration."

The Wilson Desk

C&O Desk

The C&O Desk was used in the Oval Office by George H. W. Bush, who moved it from his vice presidential office in the Capitol. It is a handsome reproduction of an eighteenth-century English double pedestal desk, with a full set of drawers on each side, made around 1920 for the owners of the Chesapeake & Ohio Railway. It was later donated to the White House and used by Ford, Carter, and Reagan in the West Wing Study.

Your Own Desk

You can, of course, bring your own desk with you to the Oval Office, as did Lyndon Johnson. The Johnson desk is now in the replica Oval Office at the LBJ museum in Austin, and, I am reliably told, the retired president sometimes sat at the desk to surprise unsuspecting museum visitors.

The C&O Desk

PRESIDENTIAL TRANSITIONS:
A STUDY APPROACH

Whether in a class or a study group, or simply quenching one's own curiosity, the transition can be an excellent focal point for examining how to construct a successful presidency.

All the pieces are there for us to put together. Presidents tell their own stories. Extensive media coverage is now available on the Internet. A remarkable number of the participants rush to write books. And there is a rich scholarship on the subject.

CHAPTER 7

Presidential Transitions

A Study Approach

If I were teaching the course, I think I might start at the end—the Inaugural Address—where the president-elect becomes the president and states his ambitions for his presidency. My students, of course, would have done their homework: they would have read the four greatest speeches—Lincoln's two, FDR's first, and Kennedy's—along with William Safire's commentary in his *Lend Me Your Ears: Great Speeches in History* (W. W. Norton, 2004).

Every course needs a spine, sometimes a textbook. The backbone of my course would be Charles O. Jones, *Passages to the Presidency: From Campaigning to Governing* (Brookings, 1998); and James P. Pfiffner, *The Strategic Presidency: Hitting the Ground Running* (2nd edition, University Press of Kansas, 1996). And, as every teacher knows, it is necessary to keep reading to stay ahead of your students. I would reread John P. Burke's two books, *Presidential Transitions: From Politics to Practice* (Lynne Rienner, 2000) and *Becoming President: The Bush Transition, 2000–2003* (Lynne Rienner, 2004).

Something that is special about transitions is that so many people are giving advice to the president-elect. It would be interesting to return to the words of these advisers to judge their skill and merit. In this category, I'd check on Richard Neustadt's memos to Kennedy, Reagan, and Clinton, as compiled by Charles O. Jones in *Preparing to Be President* (AEI Press, 2000); my own advice to Carter and Reagan, included in Stephen Hess, with James P. Pfiffner, *Organizing the Presidency* (3rd edition, Brookings, 2002); the advice to Clinton from William A. Galston and Elaine G. Kamarck in Will Marshall and Martin Schram, editors, *Mandate for Change* (Berkley Books, 1993); the George W. Bush advisers in *The Keys to a Successful Presidency* (Heritage Foundation, 2000), edited by Alvin S. Felzenberg; and Madeleine Albright's thoughts for a generic president in *Memo to the President Elect* (HarperCollins, 2008).

For an overview of White House operations, the expert is my colleague from the Eisenhower and Nixon staffs, Bradley H. Patterson Jr., who has now written his third book of virtually office-by-office deconstruction: See *To Serve the President: Continuity and Innovation in the White House Staff* (Brookings, 2008). An invaluable collection of studies by scholars is *The White House World: Transitions, Organization, and Office Operations* (Texas A&M University Press, 2003), edited by Martha Joynt Kumar and Terry Sullivan, whose contributors included Maryanne Borrelli, George C. Edwards III, Karen Hult, Nancy Kassop, Kathryn Dunn Tenpas, Charles E. Walcott, Shirley Anne Warshaw, and Stephen Wayne.

To go into more detail, there are books on different aspects of the White House. On speechwriting, there is Robert Schlesinger's lively *White House Ghosts: Presidents and Their Speechwriters* (Simon & Schuster, 2008), and an interesting collection of scholarly pieces, *Presidential Speechwriting* (Texas A&M University Press, 2003), edited by Kurt Ritter and Martin J. Medhurst. On communications operations, see Martha Joynt Kumar, *Managing the President's Message* (Johns Hopkins University Press, 2007), and John Anthony Maltese, *Spin Control* (University of North Carolina Press, 1992).

Two important books that I read in manuscript, to be published in 2009, explain how presidents should maintain the delicate balance of national security adviser/secretary of state/secretary of defense. They are (with tentative titles): Ivo Daalder and I. M. Destler, *In the Shadow of the Oval Office: The President's National Security Advisers and the Making of American Foreign Policy* (Simon & Schuster); and Peter W. Rodman, *Presidential Command* (Alfred A. Knopf).

If you wish to continue your study beyond the inauguration and into "The First Hundred Days"—which you should!—interesting short pieces on the experiences of past presidents by James MacGregor Burns, Fred I. Greenstein, Charles Bartlett, Michael Beschloss, Lee Huebner, Lou Cannon, and David Gergen can be found in *Report to the President-Elect 2000: Triumphs and Tragedies of the Modern Presidency* (Washington: Center for the Study of the Presidency, 2000), edited by David M. Abshire.

For Further Study

To understand the modern presidency, I recommend you try these three books:

- Published in 1960, written by a young professor at Columbia, Richard E. Neustadt's slim volume *Presidential Power: The Politics of Leadership* (John L. Wiley, various editions) is a scholar's immersion into the real world of power politics. Rather than offering an analysis of Article II of the Constitution or another "Great Men as History" tome, Neustadt shows how presidents operate in a fragmented system of shared authority. This is about the "art" of leadership and the "techniques" of persuasion.

- Irving L. Janis, the author of *Victims of Groupthink: A Psychological Study of Foreign-Policy Decisions and Fiascoes* (Houghton Mifflin, 1972), was a professor of psychology at Yale whose research on stress had centered on dieting and giving up smoking. But after reading Arthur Schlesinger's account of the Bay of Pigs invasion, he puzzled: "How could bright, shrewd men like John F. Kennedy and his advisers be taken in by the CIA's stupid, patchwork plan?" From this question he develops the theory of "groupthink," an explanation of the intense conformity pressures within groups making important foreign-policy decisions that limit the range of options considered, bias analysis of information, and promote simplistic stereotypes.

- Princeton Professor Fred I. Greenstein asks why presidents succeed or fail in *The Presidential Difference: Leadership Style from FDR to George W. Bush* (Princeton University Press, 2004). He measures the twelve most recent presidents on six scales: public communications, organizational capacity, political skill, vision, cognitive style, and emotional intelligence. What is necessary is the proper mix. Political skills could not save Lyndon Johnson; organizational skills did not do much for Jimmy Carter. Most important on Greenstein's list is emotional intelligence (or what I think of as "psychological wellness").

White House Assistants

For a portrait of policymaking and politics inside the White House, try these memoirs by these White House assistants:

Sherman Adams,* *Firsthand Report: The Story of the Eisenhower Administration* (Harper, 1961)

Martin Anderson, *Revolution* (Harcourt Brace Jovanovich, 1988)

Joseph A. Califano Jr., *Governing America: An Insider's Report from the White House and the Cabinet* (Simon & Schuster, 1981)

Clark Clifford, *Counsel to the President: A Memoir* (Random House, 1991)

John Ehrlichman, *Witness to Power: The Nixon Years* (Simon & Schuster, 1982)

Chester E. Finn Jr., *Education and the Presidency* (Lexington Books, 1977)

Eric F. Goldman, *The Tragedy of Lyndon Johnson* (Knopf, 1969)

H.R. Haldeman,* *The Ends of Power* (Times Books, 1978)

James R. Killian Jr., *Sputnik, Scientists, and Eisenhower: A Memoir of the First Special Assistant to the President for Science and Technology* (MIT Press, 1977)

Harry McPherson, *A Political Education* (Little, Brown, 1972)

Edwin Meese III, *With Reagan: The Inside Story* (Regnery Gateway, 1992)

Daniel P. Moynihan, *The Politics of a Guaranteed Income: The Nixon Administration and the Family Assistance Plan* (Random House, 1973)

Roger B. Porter, *Presidential Decision Making: The Economic Policy Board* (Cambridge University Press, 1980)

Donald T. Regan,* *For the Record: From Wall Street to Washington* (Harcourt Brace Jovanovich, 1988)

* Denotes chief of staff

Press Secretaries

For an insider's look at the job of press secretary, try these memoirs:

Marlin Fitzwater, *Call the Briefing! Bush and Reagan, Sam and Helen: A Decade with Presidents and the Press* (Times Books, 1995)

Ari Fleischer, *Taking Heat: The President, the Press, and My Years in the White House* (William Morrow, 2005)

Robert Ferrell, editor, *The Diary of James C. Hagerty: Eisenhower in Mid-Course, 1954–1955* (Indiana University, 1983)

Ron Nessen, *It Sure Looks Different from the Inside* (Playboy Press, 1978)

Jody Powell, *The Other Side of the Story* (William Morrow, 1984)

Pierre Salinger, *With Kennedy* (Doubleday, 1966)

Larry Speakes, *Speaking Out: The Reagan Presidency from Inside the White House* (Scribner, 1988)

Speechwriters

For an examination of life as a presidential speechwriter, give these memoirs a try:

David Frum, *The Right Man: An Inside Account of the Bush White House* (Random House, 2003)

Robert T. Hartmann, *Palace Politics: An Inside Account of the Ford Years* (McGraw-Hill, 1980)

Peggy Noonan, *What I Saw at the Revolution: A Political Life in the Reagan Era* (Random House, 1990)

Raymond Price, *With Nixon* (Viking, 1977)

Samuel I. Rosenman, *Working with Roosevelt* (Harper, 1952)

William Safire, *Before the Fall: An Inside View of the Pre-Watergate White House* (Doubleday, 1975)

Ted Sorensen, *Counselor: A Life at the Edge of History* (HarperCollins, 2008)

Michael Waldman, *POTUS Speaks: Finding the Words That Defined the Clinton Presidency* (Simon & Schuster, 2001)

Thanks

It's been a lot of fun writing this book; or, perhaps just as accurately, putting it together: a little book, but, as I hope you've noticed, complicated, a bit like a jigsaw puzzle. And now there are a lot of people to thank.

First, Strobe Talbott and Bill Antholis, president and managing director, respectively, at Brookings, for enthusiastically encouraging such an un-Brookings type of book.

Next, my colleagues in Governance Studies, under the direction of Pietro Nivola when this book was written, for creating an atmosphere of goodwill and friendship that would be shocking in some university departments; with added thanks to our support staff: Bethany Hase, Erin Carter, and Gladys Arrisueño.

To the men and women of the Brookings Institution Press, Bob Faherty, director: We have been together through books (12), revised editions (5), book chapters (6), and I continue to be amazed at the patience and understanding they give to each nattering author. On this book, my debt is to these skilled editors and designers: Janet Walker, Richard Walker, Larry Converse, Vicky Macintyre, and Debra Naylor of Naylor Design.

Three good friends, and leading presidency scholars, gave my manuscript their critical attention: Bill Galston, Chuck Jones, and Jim Pfiffner. The remaining errors are not their fault.

I'm also grateful to my friends in the cartooning world who generously let me borrow their work: Tony Auth (and Marry Suggett at United Press Syndicate), KAL (aka Kevin Kallaugher), Jimmy Margulies, Pat Oliphant, Ann Telnaes, and Frank Swoboda and Sarah Armstrong of the Herbert Block Foundation.

The Brookings Library, led by Cy Behroozi, was, as always, wonderful to me, with added thanks to research librarian Sarah Chilton.

I was blessed with four supercharged interns: Kahlie Dufresne (Dartmouth), Paul Foreman (Pomona), the tireless Andy Hanna (Northwestern and Georgetown) and Joe Berger (Catholic University).

Among the friends who answered some pointed questions along the way were Mort Abramowitz, Ken Dam, Steve Friedman, Frank Gannon, Alan Greenspan, Lee Huebner, and Bill Safire.

My appreciation to Bill Allman, curator of the White House, and thanks also to the White House Historical Association; to Mark Knoller, the CBS Radio correspondent who shared his vast knowledge of the White House press corps; the Senate Historical Office; and the many kind people who responded to requests at the Bush, Carter, Clinton, Eisenhower, Johnson, Kennedy, and Reagan libraries. The United States is well served by those who staff the presidential libraries.

Stephen Hess
September 2008

Index

Boxes are indicated by "*b*" following page numbers; illustrations, cases in point, worksheets, and examples are indicated by page numbers in italics.

Photo Credits

Page 24: Portrait of Washington, courtesy of White House Historical Association (White House Collection)

Page 25: Executive Office Building, iStock Photo

Page 42: Portrait of Washington, courtesy of White House Historical Association (White House Collection)

Page 49: Portrait of Washington, courtesy of White House Historical Association (White House Collection)

Page 76: Portrait of Jackson, Andrew W. Mellon Collection, courtesy of the Board of Directors, National Gallery of Art, Washington, D.C.

Page 94: Library of Congress

Page 100: Portrait of Lincoln, courtesy of White House Historical Association (White House Collection)

Page 118: Portrait of Roosevelt, courtesy of White House Historical Association (White House Collection)

Page 124: Eisenhower inauguration envelope, iStock Photo

Page 142: Oval Office during the Reagan administration, photo courtesy of White House Historical Association

Page 146: Oval Office during the Kennedy administration, photo courtesy of White House Historical Association

Page 152: Photo courtesy of the Ronald Reagan Library, National Archives and Records Administration

Page 153: Photo courtesy of Dwight D. Eisenhower Library, National Archives and Records Administration

Page 154: Photo courtesy of White House Historical Association

Page 155: Photo courtesy of White House Historical Association